REPORT WRITING IN ASSESSMENT AND EVALUATION

Stephen W. Thomas

Copyright © 1986

Materials Development Center
Stout Vocational Rehabilitation Institute
School of Education and Human Services
University of Wisconsin-Stout

All rights reserved. No part of this book may be reproduced or utilized in any form or by any means, electronic or mechanical, including photocopying or recording, or by any information storage or retrieval system without permission in writing from the publisher.

ISBN: 0-916671-56-9

This publication was funded in part by a grant from the Rehabilitation Services Administration, U.S. Department of Education, Washington, D.C.

PREFACE

Report writing in vocational evaluation is a process of contrasts. Although report writers have often approached the process as a challenge in presenting the most accurate picture possible of the client and his/her habilitation, rehabilitation education and/or vocational needs, writers have also viewed report writing as a boring and routine exercise, often robbing them of precious time they feel could be better spent in direct contact with the client. Report writing is not new to the human service process, and it is very doubtful that this activity will ever "go away."

In spite of the many problems experienced in writing reports about people, vocational evaluators have a great deal of influence over their clients' futures simply by what they say in a report. Some writers never truly grasp the importance of their words and recommendations on other people's lives. To these writers, I would recommend that for a few brief moments, put yourself in your clients' shoes. Imagine someone else, an evaluator just like yourself, having the power to direct your destiny with the stroke of a pen. Imagine yourself or even a close family member being written about and described in three, four, or five pages; your life determined by what is in those few pages. If you would not want someone else to write about you or a close family member in the same way you write about your own clients, then maybe you should rethink your approach to writing evaluation reports.

Many of us originally took jobs as vocational evaluators (including myself) without any formal training and, for the most part, had to learn our trade on the job at the expense of our clients. Report writing was no exception. It is disturbing to think of some of the things I said - and should not have said - about the people I served. If only I knew then what I know now, I would have written some reports differently. Unfortunately, many evaluators hired today are still untrained for their jobs. But it is hoped that with the greater availability of pre-service and in-service training, and the proliferation of more practically oriented publications, such as this one, the unconscious mistakes so often committed during report writing can be minimized. To that end, this book has been written.

For the new evaluator, this book is a step-by-step guide of how to logically and efficiently write beneficial, meaningful, and practical vocationally oriented reports. For the experienced evaluator this book will give you fresh, new approaches to organizing and saying things that may have become so routine and boring that they have reduced your willingness to write and ultimately the effectiveness of what you are trying to say.

Remember, you are more than just a report writer. You are an author of new ideas and new directions for lives that may never have had any. This one thought may help you keep a proper perspective on the critical importance of "report writing in assessment and evaluation."

Stephen W. Thomas
October, 1986

ACKNOWLEDGEMENTS

I would like to take this opportunity to sincerely thank the many people whose significant help, contributions, support, and patience made this publication a reality:

The Materials Development Center for their willingness to publish this document, and their patience throughout the long process of text preparation.

Dr. Karl Botterbusch for his skillful editing and generous support of the manuscript.

Gloria Edwards and Pennie Briley for their many long hours of excellent typing.

My wife, Melodie Thomas, and Gloria Edwards for their careful editing of the rough drafts.

My daughters Darby and Morgan, for the many evenings and weekends they gave up from me so that I could write this book.

My father-in-law, Warren H. Yoder, for the original cover design.

The many vocational evaluators, evaluation clients, and graduate students who inspired and encouraged me to write about this subject.

And the following nine vocational evaluators, their employers, and companies who so generously contributed reports for inclusion in this book:

Greenville Evaluation Program
Division of Vocational Rehabilitation Services
Greenville, North Carolina
Jim Warren, M.S., CVE, Vocational Evaluator
Jim Mullen, M.S., CVE, Evaluation Supervisor

Vocational Trades of Alamance and Caswell Counties
Burlington, North Carolina
Constance M. White, M.S., CVE, Vocational Evaluator

Northwestern Regional Vocational Assessment Center
Stephens City, Virginia
Frances G. Smith, CVE, Vocational Assessment Coordinator

Regional Vocational Assessment Center
University of Washington
Seattle, Washington
Megan Sheridan, M.S., Vocational Evaluator
Debra L. Kaplan, M.S., CRC, Vocational Evaluation Project Director

Cincinnati Evaluation Center
Cincinnati, Ohio
Paul S. Meyer, CVE, CWA, Vocational Analyst

Ellis and Associates, Incorporated
Chicago, Illinois
Debra Homa, CRC, Rehabilitation Specialist
Steven M. Blumenthal, M.S., CRC, CVE, Rehabilitation Supervisor
Cindy R. Ellis, CRC, CVE, President

Vocational Research Institute
Philadelphia, Pennsylvania
Howard Dansky, Senior Research Associate
Randy Lindsey, Director of Product Development

Career Evaluation Systems, Incorporated
Niles, Illinois
Ann Williamson, Vice President
and
Easter Seal Rehabilitation Center
San Antonio, Texas
Joe De La Cruz, Director of Rehabilitation

VALPAR International Corporation
Tucson, Arizona
Donald R. Ross, Ed.D., Vice President
Director, Product Development

                              Stephen W. Thomas
                              October, 1986

TABLE OF CONTENTS

CHAPTER		Page
I.	INTRODUCTION	1
	Defining the Vocational Evaluation Report	1
	The Ultimate Means of Communication	2
	The "Skill" of Meaningful Report Writing	3
	The "Art" of Meaningful Report Writing	3
	The "Science" of Meaningful Report Writing	4
	Conclusion	4
II.	COMMUNICATION AND AWARENESS	5
	Communicating Effectively	5
	Who are you Writing For?	5
	What do They Want?	6
	Conclusion	7
III.	CHARACTERISTICS OF GOOD REPORTS	9
	Report Length	9
	How Long Does it Take to Write a Report	11
	Report Turnaround Time	12
	What Makes a Report Good?	13
	Report Writing Tips	15
	Conclusion	17
IV.	PROBLEMS IN REPORT WRITING	19
	Burnout and Report Writing	19
	The Problem with This Report is	20
	Conclusion	23
V.	WRITING IN DIFFERENT SETTINGS	25
	Reports Vary by Setting	25
	Reports Vary by Evaluation Length	25
	What Each Setting is Designed to do	26
	Conclusion	31
VI.	DEVELOPING REPORT OUTCOME OPTIONS	33
	Defining Evaluation and Assessment by Outcome	33
	Functional Outcomes: Selected Studies of Report Recommendations	36
	The Recommendation Checklist	38
	Conclusion	39

VII.	TYPES OF EVALUATION AND ASSESSMENT REPORTS.	41
	Choosing a Report Type.	41
	The Narrative Report.	41
	The Checklist Report	42
	The Narrative Checklist	42
	Computer-Generated Reports	43
	Report Packages	44
	Conclusion.	45
VIII.	PREPARING TO WRITE A REPORT.	47
	Organizing the File	47
	Organizing the Outline	47
	Tips on Using Dictation Equipment	48
	Conclusion.	49
IX.	THE REPORT FORMAT	51
	Components of a Report.	51
	Formats by Setting	51
	A General Format.	53
	Conclusion.	57
X.	ORGANIZING THE BODY OF THE REPORT.	59
	The Organization Process	59
	The Topic Outline	59
	Performance Outcome.	59
	Chronological Order	60
	Combinations of Approaches.	60
	An Example of the Organization Process	60
	Conclusion.	61
XI.	CONTENT OF INSTRUMENT DESCRIPTION.	63
	What Goes Where?.	63
	What Should be Covered?	63
	Instrument Name	63
	Descriptions	63
	Scores	64
	Norm Groups.	65
	Behavior Observations	65
	Readministration and Modification	66
	Overall Interpretation	67
	Reporting Results: An Example	68
	Conclusion	68

XII.	WRITING PRESCRIPTIVE RECOMMENDATIONS	69
	What is a Prescriptive Recommendation	69
	List Recommendations in Priority Order	70
	Prioritize Probable Jobs, Training, and Services	70
	Separate Recommendations	71
	Use a General-to-Specifics Approach	71
	List Alternatives	72
	Specify Contingencies	72
	Use Narrative Descriptions	73
	Justify Recommendations	73
	Avoid Using Absolutes	73
	Conclusion	74
XIII.	EVALUATING YOUR REPORT	75
	When to Evaluate Your Report	75
	What Needs to be Evaluated	75
	Developing Report Evaluating Strategies	77
	Conclusion	78
BIBLIOGRAPHY		81

APPENDICES

    Appendix A: Vocational Rehabilitation Unit Report

    Appendix B: Sheltered Workshop Report

    Appendix C: Ninth Grade Student Report

    Appendix D: Twelfth Grade Student Report

    Appendix E: Social Security Report

    Appendix F: Worker's Compensation Report

    Appendix G: APTICOM Report

    Appendix H: Career Evaluation Systems Report

    Appendix I: MESA Report

Chapter 1

INTRODUCTION

Defining the Vocational Evaluation Report

Before a rational discussion of any process can transpire, the parameters for that process must first be defined. So it is also true when attempting to describe the process and the parameters of writing reports in vocational evaluation. The definition that best describes this unique report writing activity is contained in the VEWAA Glossary (Pell, Fry, and Langton, 1983) of the Vocational Evaluation and Work Adjustment Association, and reads as follows:

> Report-Vocational Evaluation - A well planned, carefully written means of communicating vital vocational information about a client. It is a studied, permanent record of significant vocational data observed as a client and an evaluator interact in various types of work or work-like situations. It puts the plan, action, findings, logic, and interpretation of the evaluation in writing. It usually includes a picture of the client's worker traits and how they compare to minimal requirements of selected jobs or work areas, physical capacities, learning ability, personal characteristics, social competence, other vocational factors, and recommendation for further services. It may also provide a prescriptive-descriptive sequence of experiences which are aimed at maximizing an individual's vocational potential. (p. 10)

Over and above this definition are the standards of practice that regulate (or specify) the content and distribution of the vocational evaluation report. The best known and most widely used of these are contained in the Standards Manual for the Commission on Accreditation of Rehabilitation Facilities (1984), which accredits vocational evaluation programs in various settings. The two standards that specifically address report writing state that:

> For each individual served in vocational evaluation, a written functional evaluation report should be prepared, properly interpreted to the individual, and disseminated in a timely fashion to the program manager, referral source, and other appropriate agencies or individuals.

> Goals of these served should be expressed as job possibilities in terminology such as job titles or job families related to existing occupations in the community. When vocational goals are not found at the time of evaluation, then nonvocational goals should be specified. (p. 52)

One final guideline for vocational evaluation report writing is contained in the Standards and Procedures Manual for Certification (Commission on Certification of Work Adjustment and Vocational Evaluation Specialists, 1986). Prior to sitting for the certification examination, applicants must first prove that they have met a specified number of "Essential Knowledge and Performance Areas," through work experience and/or education or training. One of these performance areas is related to the ability to effectively write a vocational evaluation report, and reads as follows:

> Knowledge about the process of developing vocational evaluation reports, including formatting and writing. The skills include the ability to integrate, synthesize, and interpret evaluation and other

relevant data and to provide useful recommendations to the client and referral sources related to employment, training, accommodation, adjustment, and other rehabilitation/habilitation services. The ability to effectively communicate relevant evaluation data and its meaning, through staffings and meetings, is also emphasized. (p. 11)

Even if these standards do not apply to you, they reflect important considerations and processes necessary for effective report writing. In any event, the above definition succinctly describes the content and purpose of the evaluation report and will provide the foundation for this book.

The Ultimate Means of Communication

The vocational evaluation/assessment report is the most important communication tool available to the evaluators, the referral source, and the client. What is and is not said in a report has a direct bearing on how it is used. In fact, the ultimate success of a report is not measured by its structure, readability, or correct use of the English language (all of which are definitely important), but by its utility to the referral source (Esser, 1974). This should not diminish the value of other communication tools (e.g., staffings, counseling sessions); but because it is a permanent record of student/client behaviors, results, and recommendations, it tends to have a more lasting impact on service provision.

When written descriptively, and with care, reports become a plan of action. They are a window to client/student behaviors, and an accurate record of performance. All of these reported facts and personal insights eventually guide service provision. You might even say that vocational evaluation/assessment can be defined and directed by what you can ultimately say in the report (i.e., limits on evaluation/assessment services are set by the specific recommendations you can and cannot make).

Report writing should never be taken for granted or approached with uncertainty, because in serving as a permanent record of your client/student, it also becomes (like it or not) a legal document. You become responsible and accountable for what you say. Since the report is a "product" of your agency/facility/school, it directly reflects on your collective reputation. It is an outcome by which others judge your competence and your overall evaluation and assessment skills (Coffey, 1977). For evaluators who must market their services, and whose salaries and jobs are based on their ability to generate referrals, meaningful reports serve as one of the best public relations tools. Unfortunately, poorly written reports have a dramatically opposite effect. Not only do individual referral sources stop sending clients, but word of your inadequate reports spreads to other potential referral sources who may also decide not to make referrals. Your credibility is tarnished, and in some cases, irreparably damaged. In the long run, everybody loses: the evaluator; the referral source; and worst of all, the client.

The importance of report writing in the evaluator's daily activities cannot be over-emphasized. Coffey, Hansen, Menz, and Coker (1978) analyzed results of a 175-item survey sent to 116 vocational evaluators, educators, and students nationwide. The survey was designed in part to identify the important job roles (competencies) needed by vocational evaluators in performing their duties. The highest ranking competency was, "Write evaluation reports which emphasize client strengths and needs" (p. 9).

Ellsworth and Noll (1978) analyzed 166 questionnaires received from evaluators serving vocational education students with special needs; 89% of these evaluators were employed directly in the schools. One of the areas studied, "job functions," found that 87% of the respondents had to "Prepare written work evaluation reports," which tied with two other tasks ("Score and interpret work samples, inventories, and tests" and "Communicate with outside agencies") as the most frequently performed tasks. The survey also discovered that evaluators devoted 25% of their time to report writing, which was second only to "Select and administer dexterity tests and work samples," consuming 30% of evaluators' time.

Riley (1980) conducted a survey of approximately 116 rehabilitation facilities within the Great Plains Region (i.e., the 10 states of Colorado, Iowa, Kansas, Missouri, Montana, Nebraska, North Dakota, South Dakota, Utah, and Wyoming). One part of the survey required respondents to list the key words and phrases specific to their vocational evaluator's job descriptions. The number one key word/phrase that was given by 48.8% of the respondents was "produces written reports of evaluation results" (p. 152).

A 1985 survey conducted with the VEWAA membership focused primarily on identifying major job duties and needs of vocational evaluators (Thomas, 1985). The study found that the 106 survey respondents considered report writing to be their most time-consuming, most important, and most difficult job duties.

Clearly, report writing is not only important to the referral source and the student/client in planning and providing services, but it is an equally important part of the evaluator's daily activities. There is no doubt that if vocational evaluation/assessment specialists are to provide effective goal-oriented services to their clients, then the highest priority possible should be placed on learning the skill, art, and science of meaningful report writing.

The "Skill" of Meaningful Report Writing

The most fundamental aspect of writing any kind of report is knowing the basics of good writing. A good working knowledge of vocational evaluation and interpretation must be supplemented by the essential skills needed to construct a sound sentence and paragraph, and use appropriate grammar and syntax.

Knowing how to succinctly express oneself on paper is just as important as understanding how to formulate a good recommendation. As previously mentioned, the results of poorly organized and written reports may have less credibility even if the content and recommendations are accurate. A good business, technical, or creative writing class would be of great benefit to evaluators who do not write well. All evaluators should keep a good "writing style" reference book at their desks, next to their dictionaries.

One final consideration is the skill needed in "controlling" the report. If you do not take control of the report, it will take control of you. You must not allow an outline, format, or process to dictate what, and how, something is written. Granted, there are guidelines and rules that need to be followed in writing any report, however, you are writing about a client/student so that a referral source can render pertinent services; you are not writing to satisfy a particular format or style. If what you have to say does not lend itself to a particular style, then you must be flexible enough - and willing - to change it.

The "Art" of Meaningful Report Writing

Consider that within the limited confines of your report, you are trying to "paint an accurate picture" of your client. You want to be able to render what you saw and heard into descriptive words and sentences. You want to convincingly express feelings, opinions, and impressions that translate into a workable plan of action. You must be able to creatively state ideas and demonstrate the art of good judgment. Effectively describing subjective information without "coloring" fact with prejudicial thought requires constant attention and sensitivity to the truth. The writer must be willing and able to take risks with what is said (i.e., knowing when to give the client the benefit of the doubt) and believably relate even the most questionable results to independent living, education/training, and employment. Cautiously and artistically sharing your intuition and feelings about your client or student may add a certain depth to the report, often leading to a better understanding of the client and what is needed most.

The "Science" of Meaningful Report Writing

Scientific inquiry is the precursor of sound evaluation methodology. From an applied standpoint, the ability to think and reason scientifically is an integral part of the final report-writing process. The vocational evaluator must be able to objectively and systematically write about fact and data-based results.

To a large measure, interpretations must be supported with logic and proof if referral sources are to be convinced to use the report as a credible guidance tool.

Thorough data analysis is critical to writing conclusive outcome statements. Knowledge in the proper use of scores and how to convert them into client profiles for job matching purposes is a key ingredient in formulating job options for the client. In any evaluation/assessment report, an ordered, analytical approach is essential to developing accurate and reliable recommendations, which can be arranged by their "probabilities for success."

Conclusion

Formulating a believable report requires a careful balance of subjective and objective information. This is best accomplished when the "art" and "science" of report writing are "skillfully" blended to yield a document supporting opinions with fact, and conclusions with reason. The best recipe for meaningful report writing is one of thoughtful deliberation, honest inquiry, and sensitivity to the wants and needs of others.

Chapter II

COMMUNICATION AND AWARENESS

Communicating Effectively

To a certain degree, evaluators function much like a videotape recorder. They observe and record so that they can accurately feed the information back in the form of a written report that supports their interpretations and recommendations. In this feedback process, a certain amount of editing takes place so that only the facts critical to the client/student are revealed. This editing is done for several reasons:

1. not all facts are pertinent or relevant to the case and, therefore, do not need to be presented;

2. limited space in a report may prohibit the inclusion of every fact and detail; and/or,

3. the information does not address the client's or referral source's needs.

Deciding what and what not to include in a report is a tough decision, and the evaluator may not always make the right one. Only by knowing the needs and goals of your student/client and referral source will you be able to make a more informed determination.

Frequently, reports are a summary of what was discussed and decided in a staffing. The staffing allows evaluators to share and discuss ideas, results, and potential recommendations with those in attendance. It is an important process for evaluators who need assistance in interpreting and writing up complicated, questionable, or confusing results.

The staffing can help evaluators to determine what is, and is not, important and to reinforce or to improve specific report statements or recommendations. It is often comforting to know that what you have written in a report is also the consensus of the group. This ensures that what is communicated to the referral source will, indeed, meet their needs.

As insignificant as it may seem, the title at the top of your report is important in initially specifying to the reader the original intent or purpose of the report. Titles, such as Comprehensive Vocational Evaluation Report, Vocational Assessment Report, Prevocational Evaluation Report, Report of Vocational Potential, Results of Vocational Screening, Situational Assessment Report, Physical Capacity Evaluation Report, Functional Assessment Report, and Work History Report, immediately identify what the user is about to read. In some instances, writers have used titles such as "Comprehensive Vocational Evaluation Report" when in fact only a few instruments were administered (e.g., a fifteen-minute interview and an interest test). These titles not only mislead the reader but create confusion in terms of understanding what a vocational evaluation/assessment is in actuality. Specific formats, purposes, and evaluation approaches will determine how a report should be titled.

Who are you Writing for?

An evaluation/assessment report is written for a very specific purpose: to meet the vocational needs of the student/client and the referral source. All results should primarily be related to the vocational/occupational/career aspects of the individual and not the medical or psychological implications (i.e., stay within your area of expertise). It is easy to write a medical or psychological statement; and the more you make such statements, the more liberties you begin to take. After awhile, your reports no longer sound like vocational evaluation reports. If you are not licensed to practice psychology or medicine in your state, then you may find yourself in an uncomfortable, even embarrassing situation with your report content, particularly if your report is used for forensic purposes (Field and Sink, 1981).

A vocational evaluation report should be a free-standing document (Tenth Institute on Rehabilitation Services, 1972). In other words, the content should provide sufficient detail and direction to allow the report to be used relatively independently. Although evaluation/assessment reports are often used in conjunction with other documents (e.g., medical, psychological, education, personal/reports), they should be able to serve as the primary vocational resource.

Knowing your readers, and what they expect from an evaluation/assessment report, and how they plan to use the information are essential ingredients to communicating effectively (Miller and Alfano, 1974). Thoroughly reading the referral information, answering referral questions, conducting follow-ups on students/clients, and maintaining a good working relationship (including two-way communication) with the referral source will serve to improve overall report effectiveness (Simmons, 1975). The writer must always be sensitive to the needs, and perspective, of the reader if the report is to have any value whatsoever.

Vocational evaluation/assessment reports are not protected under any laws of confidentiality. Considering the rights of access, they should always be written with the assumption that the client, family, or legal guardians will read them. In many cases, referral sources either read and explain reports to their students/clients and family, or routinely allow them to read the reports themselves. When evaluators are cognizant of this activity, it causes them to think more honestly and responsibly about how they use words, organize sentences, and explain delicate information. If you feel there is certain information in your vocational report that a student/client should not readily have access to, then maybe it should not be written, or sufficient documentation should be provided to justify why it was included and the information couched in vocational terms.

In a few instances, unexpected parties other than the student/client and referral source may have access to the report. Since a report is a legal record, it may end up being used in more ways than planned. For example, reports may be requested, or even subpoenaed, for use in social security hearings, industrial compensation or personal injury cases, criminal hearings and trials, competency and custody hearings, educational grievances and disputes, and even divorce settlements. The evaluator may also be requested to testify in order to explain or defend the content of the report. Such a potentially scary and unappealing prospect should not discourage you from including what you feel is essential information. Unfortunately, fear of legal entanglements has even prompted some evaluators to write so cautiously that the resulting report had absolutely no meaning or utility to anyone. In any event, you should write every report as though it was going to be used in court (Ellis, 1985).

What do They Want?

One of the difficult questions faced in writing a report is "How much information is enough?" The answer to this question is often determined by knowing what will be used by the referral source (VALPAR-SPECTIVE, 1975).

Do you reiterate medical, psychological, educational, and work history information that is already in the file? In this instance, it might be more appropriate to refer the reader to other documents that contain these data and use it only when it is pertinent to supporting a particular statement, interpretation, or recommendation.

When discussing tests and work samples, should descriptions of instruments and norm groups be given? Should raw scores (e.g., time, errors, correct responses) be reported along with converted scores (e.g., percentile scores, standard scores, scale scores, stanines)? This would depend on the importance of the instrument, and its outcome to the overall evaluation.

Should Dictionary of Occupational Titles (DOT) codes be listed with every job title? This would depend on how descriptive the job title is, as well as on the preference of the referral source (Simmons, 1975).

In many instances, only experience and good feedback from the referral sources will give you guidance in knowing what should be included in your reports.

Conclusion

In order for a report to convey usable information, evaluators must be acutely aware of who it is they are writing for and what they need. Although evaluation and assessment reports should have a strong vocational orientation, writers may find that the report will be used in a wider variety of settings than previously anticipated. Ultimately, report content may vary depending on the type of report being written and its overall purpose. Effective communication depends greatly on the relationship, understanding, and rapport established between the writer, reader, and client/student; these important factors have often been ignored by many unsuccessful evaluators.

Chapter III

CHARACTERISTICS OF GOOD REPORTS

Report Length

Simply stated, good reports provide usable information. Their "goodness" and utility, to a great extent, are dependent on how much quality information is included in the report. Unfortunately, the more information you include, the longer the report, and the less willing referral sources are to read it. Smith (1971), in presenting a rehabilitation counselor's perspective on vocational evaluation reports, felt that they should be limited to one or two pages in length. Attachments, such as Wechsler Adult Intelligence Scale (WAIS) and General Aptitude Test Battery (GATB) results, could also accompany the report.

Miller and Alfano (1974) conducted a study on fifty-five questionnaires returned by Tennessee Division of Vocational Rehabilitation counselors regarding their opinions on the efficacy of Tennessee's metropolitan rehabilitation facilities. One of the outcomes that specifically addressed vocational evaluation report length indicated:

> Counselors preferred that facilities limit the final report to approximately two pages in length. Given a choice of one, two, three, four, and more than four pages, the counselors requested a mean length of 2.22 pages. (p.33)

In an interview of 36 vocational rehabilitation counselors in four Georgia cities, Simmons (1975) attempted to ascertain their opinions concerning vocational evaluation reports. She found that most counselors felt evaluation reports were too long and should not exceed two pages in length.

Simmons also reviewed a 1972 unpublished study by R. S. McDaniel, that examined Alabama rehabilitation counselors' attitudes regarding vocational evaluation reports. The results indicated that 62% of the counselors surveyed thought an evaluation report should be two pages in length.

In a more recent study conducted by the Evaluation and Program Review Section of the North Carolina Division of Vocational Rehabilitation Services (NCDVRS, 1983), 100 vocational evaluation reports were randomly selected from rehabilitation counselors' files statewide for review. The three settings that generated these evaluation reports were: (1) regional rehabilitation centers (RRC) within rehabilitation hospitals primarily serving patients with head injury, stroke, and spinal cord injury; (2) Evaluation and Comprehensive Service Centers (ECSC) that are vocational evaluation units located within state vocational rehabilitation offices that generally conduct short-term evaluations; and (3) sheltered workshops (SW) that typically conduct long-term evaluations. The results of report writing length (in pages) from this study are as follows:

Unit Location	Average Report Length	Minimum Length	Maximum Length
RRC	3.2	2.0	4.3
ECSC	3.2	0.5	30
SW	3.9	1.5	10

It is no surprise that, on the average, vocational evaluation reports in sheltered workshops were the longest, since clients did spend more evaluation time in this setting than the other two.

The literature tends to consistently indicate that counselors prefer evaluation reports that are approximately two pages or less in length. However, the NCDVRS study demonstrates that, in reality, many reports average slightly over three pages. There also appears to be a contradiction in what rehabilitation counselors want in terms of report length and report content. Although counselors stated a preference for a one- to two-page report, they also felt that reports needed additional content in five general areas:

1. a more adequate interpretation of test scores (Simmons, 1975);

2. more specific and objective behavior descriptions (Simmons, 1975);

3. greater justification and support (i.e., reason and logic) for the vocational objectives and recommendations presented (Miller and Alfano, 1974; Smith, 1971);

4. a wider variety of alternative recommendations and plans (Miller and Alfano, 1974; Simmons, 1975); and,

5. "... more usable information on the client's readiness to work ..." (Miller and Alfano, 1974, pp. 36-37).

This conflict between what counselors want (shorter reports) and what they need (more documentation and alternative plans) can only be resolved by deciding what will be in the client's best interests. To this end, length should be sacrificed for quality content. Evaluators would be better criticized for writing reports that were too long than for reports that did not give enough information to help provide essential services to the student or client. Unfortunately, the hazard in writing longer reports is that users may be more prone to skim rather than read them, thus missing pertinent detail that could be critical to the success of the case.

Here are some simple rules that can help to minimize report length.

1. Information already in the referring agent's possession (e.g., background information) should not be repeated in great detail (Simmons, 1975). Only enough data should be given to identify the person you are writing about, or, as previously mentioned, used only when it is needed to support specific report content and recommendations.

2. Eliminate redundant and superfluous detail and minutiae from the report (Smith, 1971). Rereading reports prior to final typing with the specific goal of editing out repetitive statements and unnecessary verbiage will, in the long run, teach the evaluator how to think and write concisely.

3. Incorporate an appendix section at the end of your report (Smith, 1971). Instrument and norm group descriptions, raw and converted scores, and descriptive tables and charts can be added as supplements or attachments to the report. This cuts down on the amount of information needed in the body of the report (attachments will be discussed later in the book).

The length of evaluation reports used specifically for public vocational rehabilitation services will more than likely vary by setting, by the type and comprehensiveness of the referral questions asked, by the length of time the client or patient spends in that setting, and by the amount of information obtained. Vocational evaluators should not feel uncomfortable with reports that average as many as five or six quality pages (excluding appendices) as long as the content lends support and direction to the individual's total rehabilitation plan.

While vocational assessment reports used in educational settings may vary in length for the same reasons stated above, they may also vary based on when, in the student's educational experience (e.g., seventh/eighth grade, twelfth, post-secondary), the assessment is offered. Report length may not be any different than it is for vocational rehabilitation programs. However, in some school settings, report content and subsequent length have been limited strictly to what is available to the student within the confines of his or her own school.

Reports in private-for-profit (or proprietary) evaluation settings generally have more flexibility in terms of length. Evaluation reports written for forensic or legal purposes (frequently for attorneys) are more concerned with detailing fact and documentation than with minimizing length. In some cases, seven, eight, or even nine pages are not considered inappropriate. However, this does not mean that all proprietary evaluation reports should be lengthy. In fact, there are hazards inherent in writing longer reports in any setting. Longer reports take more time to write and may accelerate evaluator burnout. They are more prone to redundancy; also, the more you write, the greater your chances of including contradictory statements. These contradictions can create a nightmare during cross-examination as the report can effectively be used against the evaluator in attempting to discredit his or her testimony (Field and Sink, 1981). On the other hand, reports written for insurance adjusters may be no different in length than those written for public rehabilitation counselors. Adjusters, like VR counselors, often have large case loads and do not always have the time to read voluminous reports. Therefore, brevity and conciseness would be the rule; however, communication with referral sources on desired report length should be pursued.

Whether in a comprehensive rehabilitation facility, innovative school system, or large proprietary rehabilitation agency, any vocational evaluator providing services on a professional team concept may find that report writing is a cooperative effort. In this case, the combination of information from various disciplines (e.g., vocational evaluation/assessment, psychological testing, occupational or physical therapy) will create a rather lengthy but very cohesive and usable report (VALPAR-SPECTIVE, 1975).

How Long Does it Take to Write a Report?

Nothing seems to take longer than writing your first evaluation/assessment report. I have known a few evaluators who said they took up to eleven hours to write their first report. Writing these first few client/student reports can be a rather difficult and threatening experience (VALPAR-SPECTIVE, 1975). Time, experience, and modern technology will reduce your writing time.

Many evaluators write their first few reports by hand. Once they have mastered the process and subtleties of this uniquely demanding form of writing, other mediums are enlisted (e.g., dictation, word processing) to increase reporting speed. Handwritten reports take the longest time to complete. Time to write depends on the complexity and length of the report and the speed of the writer; they may generally take between two to four hours. Composing and typing a report will depend on typing speed, as well as on the same considerations found in handwriting reports.

Report-writing time is substantially reduced when a dictaphone is used. Again, depending on the complexity and comprehensiveness of the report, total dictation time may take between forty-five minutes to an hour.

Evaluators who compose reports on a word processor, a popular use of computers in rehabilitation today, (Blakemore, McCray, and Coker, 1985) are limited partly by their typing speed and ability to master the word processing software. Although time may not be substantially improved over the time it takes in composing a report on an electric typewriter, the ultimate time savings is realized in the ease in making minor corrections or even major revisions in a report. Tips on the use of a dictaphone or word processor will be discussed later. Many commercial work sample systems have developed report writing software dedicated to their particular battery of instruments. Results are entered into a computer and a report is printed out in a matter of minutes. Although this is one of the fastest methods of writing a report, its strengths and weaknesses will be discussed in more detail later.

One must remember that report writing time is not limited strictly to how long it takes to compose the actual document. Of equal importance is the planning and preparation time needed prior to writing to decide what it is you want to say as well as the time required to type the report and proof it for correctness, continuity, accuracy, and soundness. You may also find that revision and retyping will be required. Do not send out a report that you or your referral source may not like. The small amount of time it will take to improve your report may make the difference in the perceived reputation of you and your service.

Report Turnaround Time

Report turnaround time refers to how many days it takes from the date the client or student exits evaluation to the date the report is received by the referral source. One criticism made concerning evaluation services is that the reports are often received too late (McDaniel, 1972; Miller and Alfano, 1974; Simmons, 1975). Miller and Alfano found that it took an average of 2.07 weeks for a counselor to receive a report from a rehabilitation facility after the client had exited. This inordinately delayed the determination of client eligibility, the timely development of plans, and the expedient implementation of appropriate services. Similarly, Simmons' survey revealed that 31% of the rehabilitation counselors surveyed felt that "evaluation reports were often received late (i.e., more than two weeks after the evaluation was completed)" (p. 26). Further, these same counselors also recommended that there should be no more than a one-week turnaround time for evaluation reports.

As a rule, report turnaround time should be negotiated and included in any evaluation/assessment service contract or agreement. It should also be included in any program evaluation process since meeting the deadlines specified in a contract ultimately impacts on user satisfaction and long-term marketing success. Some evaluation/assessment units may be able to maintain a report turnaround time of less than a week, even a few days. This may be necessary in short-term vocational evaluation or screening processes that, by their very short-term nature, require an immediate report turnaround. A 72-hour turnaround time was reported in proprietary evaluations where the client was found not feasible. This allowed for the immediate discontinuation of temporary disability payments and a more expeditious final settlement (Matheson, 1985).

However, some evaluation/assessment units that are long-term in nature, or collect a large amount of information that needs to be detailed in the report, may take up to two weeks in turnaround time. In units where there is a typing backlog, reports that are written quickly still may not be sent out in less than two weeks unless significant changes in staffing patterns, typing priorities, or paper work flow can be effected. If a referral source wants a shorter turnaround time than you can offer, then negotiation for more time, a modification of the report preparation process, or a combination of the two would need to be implemented before an evaluation/assessment could be offered. For those units where report turnaround time cannot be shortened, conducting a staffing with the referral source immediately after client or student exit is recommended as an alternative means of sharing evaluation results with those who plan to use them. This will provide users with timely information that can be immediately incorporated into planning and service provision. It will also give the writer feedback in terms of what the user wants from an evaluation report, which will insure that what is written (based on staffing outcomes) will be meaningful and appropriate in meeting the student's or client's needs.

Although a unit may have an acceptable report turnaround time, there are always exceptions. The need for a quick evaluation and report for use in a legal case or a special student or client circumstance may require an immediate turnaround. However, do not let referral sources take regular advantage of this unique circumstance (i.e., where the exception becomes the rule) or they will grow to <u>expect</u> this kind of service. Not allowing yourself time to think about what you are writing could result in the production of reports that do not reflect you (or your client's) true skill and ability. Some evaluators even wait a day after writing a report before they proof it. This gives them a fresh perspective so they can objectively identify areas that need to be improved or information that needs to be added, which was inadvertently left out during the initial writing.

Regardless of the length of report turnaround, evaluators should always strive to keep this process to a minimum without negatively affecting the quality of the report. Although no specific turnaround time can be recommended, the literature tends to indicate that two weeks or less would be appropriate.

What Makes a Report Good?

To determine what truly makes a good report, one must survey those who use evaluation/assessment reports. As stated earlier, before writing a report the evaluator must determine what the referral source needs and wants and attempt to provide them with the appropriate information. Not only should a report be realistic and useful (Williams, 1975), but it should be written in a manner that would allow the reader to more readily visualize the client/student as an individual (North Carolina Division of Vocational Rehabilitation Services, 1983). Williams (1975, p. 15) also found that:

> Of the DVR counselors surveyed, 82 percent felt the recommendations were helpful in planning for and placing their clients. The counselors tended to indicate that evaluators' recommendations were helpful for the following reasons:
>
> 1. recommendations supported or documented the tentative plan the counselor had made;
>
> 2. they provided new or additional information about the client and his abilities; and
>
> 3. they located appropriate job and/or training areas for the client...

The North Carolina Division of Vocational Rehabilitation Services (1983) reviewed 100 randomly selected reports that had been generated in three different vocational evaluation settings: vocational rehabilitation unit offices (short-term evaluations/screenings), regional rehabilitation hospitals, and sheltered workshops. This study was unique in that it identified report strengths by setting. "Report recommendations" were rated most useful in the vocational rehabilitation (VR) evaluation reports, while rehabilitation hospital reports were rated most useful in their "summary and recommendations" sections. Sheltered workshop reports were rated most useful for their "behavior observations."

The study also found that the content of referral questions and the reason for referral influenced not only where a client was referred for services but what was ultimately said (and used) in a report. Counselors generally referred clients for VR evaluations when they were interested in the client's training and education needs, aptitude, achievement, interest, and intelligence. Workshops and hospital referral questions were primarily geared to identifying job areas, behavior, physical capacity, and independent living. Generally speaking, VR evaluators were being asked to provide a vocational <u>diagnosis</u>, while workshops and hospital evaluators were being asked to give a vocational <u>prognosis</u>. There was a tendency for VR evaluation reports to be used for vocational goal development, workshop evaluation reports to be used for identifying services required, and hospital evaluation reports to be used for counseling and guidance. However, overall evaluation reports were most frequently used to develop vocational goals and identify services required.

Regardless of evaluation setting, 82% of the VR counselors surveyed referred to evaluation reports in the development of their Individualized Written Rehabilitation Plans (IWRP). Eighty-four percent of the surveyed counselors generally referred to reports to assist with counseling and guidance. <u>All</u> evaluation reports were used to help: (1) plan additional services and (2) establish vocational objectives.

In other studies, rehabilitation counselors provided feedback regarding what constituted a good report, and they are as follows:

1. extensive documentation and justification should be given to support recommendations (Miller and Alfano, 1974);

2. usable information on the client's readiness to work should be provided (Miller and Alfano, 1974);

3. objective and specific behavior observation descriptions must be included (Simmons, 1975);

4. the local job (and training) market should be considered when formulating and making recommendations (Simmons, 1975);

5. a variety of alternative job and training recommendations should be presented, and not limited strictly to training or services available in the facility (or school) where the evaluation took place (Simmons, 1975); and,

6. information already known by the referral source should not be reported in great detail (Simmons, 1975).

In addition to knowing how to specifically organize and present vocational evaluation and assessment data, one must also be able to write clearly. Regardless of what it is you are writing, there are some universal report-writing guidelines that have direct application to the "readability" of our reports. Esser (1974), in illustrating the techniques necessary to write clearly, adapted Robert Gunning's (1953) principles used in "cutting through the fog."

1. <u>Keep your average sentence length short</u>. Some report-writers have a tendency to ramble on within a single sentence. A sentence should convey a single thought or two closely related thoughts. Twenty words or less is a guideline to follow, with sentences containing fifteen or sixteen words being preferable.

2. <u>Vary your sentence length</u>. Sentences all relatively the same length make for rather tedious reading. Paragraphs containing numerous short sentences result in a busy, "machine gun" style. Put some variety in your writing by using sentences of different length.

3. <u>Prefer the simple to the complex</u> and 4. <u>Prefer the familiar to the farfetched</u>. These two are very similar, and in rehabilitation reporting are probably most closely related to the excessive use of jargon. Choose the common, familiar everyday word when you can. Some writers attempt to impress the reader with their knowledge. The writer should never attempt to write in depth about things with which he is not familiar. This is not a serious likelihood in rehabilitation report writing.

5. <u>Use active verbs whenever possible</u>. The use of the active voice helps cut down on wordiness and monotony. Active verbs put vigor into writing. Example: Instead of: There are certain behaviors which limit . . .

   Say: Certain behaviors limit . . .

6. <u>Avoid unnecessary words</u>. Use as few words as you can to say what you have to say. There is seldom, if ever, a good reason for using twenty words to express something which can be stated just as well in ten. Knowing what you want to say helps in avoiding this problem.

7. <u>Use descriptive words when possible</u>. The use of active verbs as in principle #5 is helpful in descriptive writing. General statements are more effective when supported by specific facts. Behavior observations are generally good examples of descriptive statements.

8. <u>Relate your writing to the reader's experience</u>. This is not a serious problem in rehabilitation reporting since both the writer and reader are working within the same contextual framework. This does not mean, however, that information should be omitted because you assume that the reader already knows it.

9. <u>Write as you talk</u>. For some, this is a good idea; for others, probably not. This can be restated as, "write as you should talk." Verbal communication is usually more efficient than written because of voice inflections, and the opportunity to question if the meaning isn't clear. The goal in written communication is to express ideas and information as clearly as possible so that questions are minimal. In this sense, "writing as you talk" is a goal to try to achieve.

10. <u>Write to express rather than to impress</u>. Although this has already been mentioned, self-centeredness in writing is a problem with many otherwise good report writers. This happens when the writer becomes preoccupied not with what he is trying to say, but with how he is trying to say it. (pp. 6-7)

Report Writing Tips

There are a few simple report writing tips that, if followed, can improve the clarity and soundness of the content.

1. <u>Maintain a good balance</u>. This is what Esser (1974) refers to as "tone" or "attitude." It is important to present a balance of both positive and negative information so that the report does not sound unduly biased. The report is designed to <u>serve</u> the student or client, and this process would only be impaired if one-sided information is presented. We are all subject to errors in judgment (e.g., halo effect, logical error, contrast error); and writing objectively, with the goal of helping even the most "difficult" individual, will hopefully minimize these errors.

2. <u>Use the third person</u>. Writing in the third person is the generally preferred method of communicating in a professional document. Although some evaluators have been able to successfully write reports in the first person, the third person approach is easier to write, is often perceived as being more objective, and is more frequently used. Evaluators who are new to report writing may want to consider initially writing in the third person. Once they have mastered this approach and feel comfortable with the report writing process, then they can experiment with other writing styles.

3. <u>Write in the past tense</u>. In many, but not all cases, it is important to describe what happened during assessment or evaluation (past tense), before relating this information to where the client is now (present tense), or where she/he could be in the future (future tense). For example, your evaluee may be poorly groomed during evaluation and should be so stated, "Mary <u>had</u> oily hair and body odor throughout the three-day evaluation." A less appropriate wording might be "Mary <u>has</u> oily hair and body order." Although the latter might be correct, you are making an assumption without knowing how the individual looks <u>after</u> exiting the evaluation. Once a past tense statement has been made, then future needs and consequences can be safely stated, "Mary had oily hair and body odor throughout the three-day evaluation. If she is to be considered for employment as a bank teller, then her potential problems with grooming will need to be corrected." Likewise, test and work sample scores should be stated in the past tense so that vocational diagnosis and prognosis can be stated in the present and future tenses respectively.

4. <u>Do not use absolutes unless absolutely sure</u>. As with death and taxes, almost nothing in vocational evaluation or assessment is absolute. As a result of the rapid advancements in rehabilitation technology, the handicapping conditions of many disabilities are being overcome daily. Numerous clients who were thought to be unable to successfully complete training or find and maintain employment have proven their evaluation reports wrong. In an age where liability suits have reached epidemic proportions, many evaluators need to rethink how they write about the abilities and inabilities of their students and clients. Presenting levels of success in terms of probabilities, or priority order, is an effective way of dealing with the problem of absolutes. This problem is particularly important when writing recommendations. Rather than emphatically stating, "John will <u>never</u> be able to work as a secretary," it might be best to say, "Based on the above results, it is felt that John's probability for employment as a secretary is low," or "John's ability to be competitively employed as a secretary is questionable at this time, due to his . . .," or "Until John is able to . . . it is felt placement as a secretary should be given a low priority." Using words like "may" instead of

"can," and "questionable" instead of "cannot" would minimize the error of making absolute statements. However, writers must be careful not to use too many neutral or innocuous words or statements for fear the report may not say anything at all. For example, "It is possible that there is some question that John may have difficulty being considered for a potential position related to secretarial type work." Not only is this writer overly cautious in making a more definitive statement about John's low placement probability, but he/she is equally tentative in identifying the specific job in question.

5. <u>Stay within your area of expertise</u>. As previously mentioned, this is a vocational and not a medical or psychological report. Avoid statements or diagnosis that you are not licensed, certified, or legally allowed to make (Field and Sink, 1981). Do not go "overboard" with predictions or "big guesses" that you cannot support. Know the bound of what you can and cannot say.

Conclusion

In characterizing good reports, evaluators must first concentrate on meeting referral sources' needs in the fewest pages possible. Thorough documentation and a wide range of sound recommendations will increase a report's utility. Further, report-writing length is often dictated not only by what the referral source wants but by the setting in which the report is written (with sheltered workshop reports generally being the longest). The amount of time it takes to write a report is determined, in part, by its length and by the technology used (e.g., written by hand or dictated), and should include not only the time to write it but the time to prepare, proof, and revise it.

Chapter IV

PROBLEMS IN REPORT WRITING

Burnout and Report Writing

Vocational evaluators often experience burnout in the process of report writing. Burnout may not always be the result of report length or the time it takes to write the report, but of the lack of time available on the job to write. Unfortunately, meeting report writing deadlines is frequently a weak area for evaluators. All too often, evaluators find themselves taking reports home to play "catch up" during evening hours. A steady diet of report writing during off-work hours (even if one is paid) could be unhealthy to on-the-job motivation.

To counter these potential problems, specific report writing time must be set aside. When evaluators attempt to write reports at the same time they are administering work samples and tests, clients may not receive the necessary attention and assistance they require. Critical observations are missed, and pertinent information is lost. Further, continuity in report writing is broken, as is the evaluator's train of thought, since the process must be frequently interrupted to work with evaluees. This may lead to choppy, awkward wording and sentence structure that could affect the logical flow of the report. By setting aside time everyday (one or two hours) or each week (half day to full day) depending on the number of reports that need to be written, report writing during evaluation time or off-work hours can be minimized.

Regularly writing reports for a specific population (e.g., individuals who are mentally retarded), a particular setting (e.g., sheltered workshops, high schools), or a small community having limited services and job opportunities can also result in report writing burnout. In these types of settings and situations, the writer may be restricted in what can be said. After a period of time, evaluation reports start sounding alike (the "rubber stamp report") due to the limited number of instruments and techniques that can be used and the limited number of recommendations that can be made. Eventually, referral sources may start to complain that your reports appear to say the same thing about every individual (Simmons, 1975).

Vocational evaluators who have been writing reports for an extended period of time may tend to lose perspective of what they are saying. They may begin to feel that no one is even reading their reports. As a result, writers become careless; the process loses its meaning; and the report, itself, fails to meet the readers' needs. Report writing burnout results. This long-term decline in effective report writing is so subtle that many evaluators may not even recognize what is happening.

There are two suggestions to minimize report writing burnout.

1. Identify someone who can occasionally, if not regularly, proof and critique your reports. Peer review and feedback is one of the best ways to stay in touch with report quality. An experienced user of reports (e.g., counselors, teachers, placement specialists), and administrator/supervisor (particularly one who has previously been an evaluator or who is very familiar with the process), or another evaluator could adequately review your reports. If an evaluator is available, you may want to return the favor and review their reports. This may stimulate new ideas for writing such as specific wording, report formatting, organization, recommendations, or supplements.

2. Vary your report writing outline. Although changing your report writing format may extend writing time, it does provide a new perspective on how to organize and present your material. Most evaluators maintain a "general" report outline but make occasional variations to tailor the data to a particular outcome. Time and efficiency do not permit a different format for each report. However, changing your "general" outline every six months to a year may keep your reports from becoming stale, as well as help maintain reader interest.

The Problem with this Report is...

Just as a chain can be no stronger than its weakest link, reports may be judged not by their strengths but by their perceived weaknesses. What may in fact be a highly useful report will go unused if it is considered to have problems. Esser (1974), specifically addressed these problems with report writing as follows:

1. Failure to answer referral questions or provide desired information. This is perhaps one of the most serious errors in rehabilitation reporting. As already noted, the referring counselor expects certain information from the facility or workshop. If the facility does nothing else, it should strive to answer those questions or reasons for referral asked or stated by the referring counselor. On the other hand, the referring counselor has the responsibility to state the specific reasons why he is referring his client for services as well as the information that he is seeking from the facility. This mutual obligation is referred to by Gust (1967) as "reciprocal referral responsibility."

2. "Too long!" is a common complaint about narrative reports. The report should not be any longer than necessary in order to convey essential information about the client. This becomes a serious problem when it is difficult for the reader to pull out the information in which he is most interested. Detailed information is often interesting, but only up to a certain point. There should be balance between specifics and generalities, brevity and thoroughness.

3. Telling the counselor what he already knows. Some report writers have a tendency to take the referral information, rehash it, and then give it back to the referring counselor in slightly different form. This does not necessarily mean that the facility has not done its job, but it may mean that the report writer is relying too heavily on the referral information in organizing his report. This can stem from lack of confidence in his ability to write reports, or could also be an indication of a failure in internal communication among facility staff. This problem can also originate from the other end as a result of an inappropriate referral or lack of clearly stated reasons for the referral by the referring counselor or agency.

4. Failure to use referral information. This is somewhat the opposite of the last problem. Many facilities want as much referral information as they can possibly get on the client, but then fail to use it in implementing services. This is likely to show up in the report. For example, in reading the report, the referring counselor may notice that the facility

staff has not considered important information about the client. Such information could include a medical specialist's report indicating a client's inability to work in dusty conditions. Failure to read the referral information can result in embarrassing and sometimes hazardous situations. Occurrences like this can diminish a counselor's confidence in the facility.

A detailed summary of the client's history is seldom necessary. However, information pertinent to the client's vocational potential provides the reader with a reference point for understanding the report.

5. <u>The presence of contradictions in the report</u>. Human behavior is extremely complex and often contradictory. If contradictions exist in the report, this is likely to be confusing to the reader. Although apparent contradictions may occasionally arise, these should be explained if possible.

6. <u>Reluctance to present realistic or negative findings</u>. Due to a "halo effect," some report writers simply have a difficult time saying anything negative about anyone. Although it is generally good to be positive, it is also necessary to be objective. The direct opposite may also occur in that some writers may tend to emphasize only the negative qualities of their clients. Reports written completely from either the positive or negative perspective are likely to have diminished value for the reader. Report formats which are organized to present a client's limitations as well as assets are helpful in counteracting either possibility.

7. <u>Failure to backup plans and recommendations with facts and reasons</u>. Recommendations made for the client should be substantiated by facts contained within the report. In other words, it is not sufficient to state, "Mike has potential to be successful as an arc welder," unless supported by facts and reasons. Such statements without qualifying information have little meaning by themselves.

8. <u>Pure evaluation</u>. This refers to the presentation of facts and findings without any interpretation of the same by the writer. This problem really depends on the reader's viewpoint. Some counselors prefer a presentation of facts and findings so that they can draw their own conclusions and make their own interpretations. Others feel that they are paying for the writer's impressions and interpretations, particularly if they have found through experience that they can trust the writer's judgment. The real key here once again appears to be the writer's objectivity. Interpretations and impressions should be based on observable facts and findings.

9. <u>Making unrealistic plans for the client</u>. Some report writers tend to write in a vacuum. In other words, they write within the context of their own facility or workshop, failing to take the client's real world and the world of work into consideration. It is the

writer's responsibility to know his subject. Evaluation and training reports should be written in a vocational context. The report writer, therefore, has to be familiar with the employment market, training opportunities, vocational and trade schools, public transportation, and numerous other factors which may affect the client's vocational potential.

10. <u>Failure to consider alternatives</u>. Very few clients, if any, are limited to a single vocational objective or course of action. Alternatives should be presented in case the preferred objective is for some reason not available or is delayed. Some facility counselors and evaluators develop a "set" which they apply to a majority of their clients. For example, one evaluator may tend to regard most his clients as sheltered workers; another may tend to see all his female clients as potential nurses aides and his male clients as janitors. Because the referring counselor usually works with a large caseload, he may not be aware of this practice on the part of some report writers. In addition, the person preparing the report, for one reason or another, may not be conscious of his own tendency to do this. Facilities and workshops providing client-centered services in which the client plays a major part in his own rehabilitation program are not likely to fall into this rut.

11. <u>A summary which isn't</u> - The summary is one of the most important sections of the report because it is likely to be of the most benefit to the reader. The summary brings the information contained in the report together and serves as an abstract for the reader. It is the summary which provides a composite picture of the client. Some persons naturally read the summary first, even when it is located at the end of the report. Because of its importance, the summary should consist of more than a few brief lines.

12. <u>Brevity</u>. Reports should be concise and to the point. However, this can be carried to a fault. If reports are written only to fulfill a contractual requirement rather than to inform, the writer is likely to take the easy way out. The resulting reports are likely to be brief and sketchy, and of limited use to the reader.

These twelve items represent some of the major problems with reports as seen from the perspective of the reader. The list is by no means complete, but it does cover those items which are most likely to affect the usefulness of the report for the person who receives it. (pp. 2-4)

Beyond the issues of report burnout and the twelve problems identified by Esser, additional weaknesses of major and minor importance were isolated through research and surveys on report writing.

1. Smith (1971, p. 191) stated a common problem with evaluation reports is that "... they present tons of minutiae so that one is not able to draw any conclusions when he is finished reading a report..." Extensive detail in a report can add to its utility as long as the important

elements are drawn together into a concise interpretation and workable plan of action.

2. "The report creates a clear image of the client for the reader" received the lowest rating of nine important quality indicators in a random review of 100 vocational evaluation reports by the Evaluation and Program Review staff of the North Carolina Division of Vocational Rehabilitation Services (1983, p. 9) After a report is finished, the author must be able to sit back and say, "Does my report paint an accurate picture of my client for a reader who may never have met this person?" If the answer is "no," then the report is not complete. The reader must be able to visualize the student's appearance, behavior, and activity through what is written.

3. "Twenty percent of the counselors" surveyed by Simmons (1975, p. 26) "indicated that test scores were reported without being adequately interpreted." To expand on Esser's concept of "Pure evaluation" presented earlier, evaluators who do not have time to write, who evaluate too many clients, or who do not know how to relate their findings to functional outcomes may tend to only list a score and leave the interpretations to the reader. Some referral sources may be able to do this; but if evaluators are incapable or unwilling to interpret scores on tests and work samples, then they can very easily be replaced by aides or computers.

4. There is a lack of specificity in behavioral observations of the client in some evaluation reports (Simmons, 1975). It is particularly important that observed behaviors be detailed and interpreted when recommendations for work adjustment and related services are being considered.

5. Miller and Alfano (1974, p. 36) found that ". . . counselors indicated a need for more usable information on the client's readiness to work. . ."

6. ". . . the work evaluation fails to take into account the aspects of transportation that can be a severe problem for the physically disabled, the mentally retarded, and the handicapped who live in remote geographic areas not served by bus lines," was noted by Smith (1971, p. 191) as another common problem. In addition, failure to consider issues of accommodation, communication, and family support when writing recommendations can result in unanticipated problems with successful placement.

7. Recommendations were unrealistic and inadequate. To expand upon Esser's reasons (i.e., writing in a vacuum), Williams (1975) found that recommendations tended to be least effective in sparsely populated rural areas. Simmons (1975) found that job recommendations were either too narrow or too broad in scope, or limited to training only available at the evaluator's facility.

8. As previously discussed in Chapter III, but worth brief reiteration, is the fact that reports were often received too late (McDaniel, 1972; Miller and Alfano, 1974; Simmons, 1975).

Although a wider array of report writing problems could be detailed, those presented here appear to be the areas where evaluators and assessment specialists should be the most sensitive. As minor as the problems may seem to the writer, it is the reader who is the final judge; and their opinions should be given attention. Failure to do so could result in a loss of credibility as well as referrals.

Conclusion

Daily report writing has its ups and downs. As Esser (1974, p. 2) puts it,

"No one writes perfect reports all of the time." But when a writer can be sensitive to the problems of reports and the needs of the reader, then these problems can be minimized and report utility maximized. Constant attention to quality calls for involving others in the review of your reports. This will prevent the author from becoming complacent and eventually burning out. Keeping in touch with what you write and how you write it will also keep you in touch with those you serve. If you receive report feedback from referral sources, use it; if you do not receive feedback, ask for it.

Chapter V

WRITING IN DIFFERENT SETTINGS

Reports Vary by Setting

Although vocational evaluation reports should strive to relate results to employment, both the evaluation/assessment goals and what we can say in a report may vary by setting. Each evaluation setting is set up to meet specific assessment needs (vocational rehabilitation needs, school needs, placement alternatives, financial settlements), and some settings may attempt to meet a number of needs. In any event, a setting may specialize its efforts; and as a result, it will attempt to organize and present the report content and recommendations in such a way that the referral source can easily understand and readily incorporate the results in planning and service. As repeatedly stated, no matter how well written and organized an evaluation report may be, if it does not address the reader's needs, then it has served as no more than an academic exercise for those involved.

However, this does not infer that cross-setting evaluations are inappropriate. In fact, if an evaluation unit takes steps to learn about the specific settings in which the reports will be used, then their utility and overall user satisfaction can be increased. For example, Cohen and Berman (1984) initiated a study to compare vocational evaluations conducted on Pittsburgh Public School District (PPSD) students, both at the school and at a local vocational rehabilitation facility. The results of the evaluations were used to place handicapped students into one of the PPSD's 45 mainstream high school vocational courses. One part of the study surveyed the counselors' opinion of the usefulness of the evaluation reports in working with students. The PPSD reports were considered to be significantly more useful (p.<.05) than the rehabilitation facility reports. Overall, however, the rehabilitation facility reports were still considered to have sufficient utility to warrant continued evaluations of the students at the local rehabilitation facility. Report utilization in similar types of cross-evaluation settings, as was true in the PPSD study, can be enhanced when the evaluators:

1. visit referral agents and programs (e.g., schools, sheltered workshops, community worksites) where the student/client will be placed after assessment, and

2. conduct follow-up surveys, visits, and staffings with referral agents to ensure that the final reports are meeting their needs.

Reports Vary by Evaluation Length

In recent years, improved assessment technologies, as well as funding restrictions in education and rehabilitation services, have brought about a reduction in the length of evaluation services. Although not everyone needs a long-term evaluation, "The philosophy of having each person reach their maximum potential has been replaced by a new pragmatic concept of evaluation to assess current skills and to provide direct placement" (Botterbusch, 1983, p.1).

Frequently, short-term evaluations are _diagnostic_ in nature. That is, they use limited amounts of information, which can be obtained from a file review, intake interview, and some rapid assessments (e.g., psychometric tests and brief work samples) to determine where the client is at present. These results, obtainable in as little as three hours, are best suited to immediate job placement.

The prognostic aspect of a long-term evaluation allows for a more comprehensive assessment of the individuals' long-term needs, which would ultimately lead to placement. In cases where the vocational diagnosis of a short-term evaluation fails to identify immediate job placement options, a longer evaluation, or vocational prognosis, could specifically explore and recommend various services (e.g., work adjustment, education, remediation, modification), which would eventually result in employment. Unfortunately, diagnostic evaluations have attempted to yield prognostic information (Nadolsky, 1985). This problem has long existed, and its abuse is on the increase with the growing popularity of short-term evaluations. Authors of assessment reports should constantly ask themselves if the evaluation, and resulting data, lends itself to a diagnostic or prognostic write-up. If the diagnostic results indicate that prognostic information will be needed before specific vocational options and directions can be generated, then a recommendation for further assessment should be rendered.

It is important to remember that vocational diagnosis and prognosis relate to more than just the issue of evaluation length. Conceptually, they represent different philosophies that direct the goals and processes of assessment and the resulting interpretations, of which length is only one part. Although this chapter has devoted considerable attention to the issue of evaluation length and its relationship to diagnosis and prognosis, their value to other aspects of evaluation should not be overlooked.

What Each Setting is Designed to Do

The following sections will give a basic overview of the focus of vocational evaluation/assessment reports by the setting in which they are written. Chapter VI will provide more detail on the specific recommendations.

Short-Term Evaluations - These rapid assessments often resemble prevocational evaluations. They are designed to provide basic vocational diagnostic information related to a person's interest, dexterity, aptitude, and achievement. Reports may be geared to eligibility determination and identifying the individual's basic need for rehabilitation, remediation, and education services. A basic transferability of skills assessment may also be reported. Answering specific and simple referral questions (e.g., could client be employed in an entry-level file clerk position?) and recommending immediate job placement possibilities are often goals of the short-term vocational evaluation report. On occasion, the need for a long-term evaluation might be the most appropriate recommendation in a short-term report.

Long-Term Evaluations - The extensive and detailed reports generated through this vocational prognostic process are designed to identify specific habilitation/rehabilitation needs of the client. A variety of program and employment options is presented that can be used in comprehensive and long-range plan development. Unique to the long-term evaluation report is the ability to explicitly detail vocational behaviors related to frequency, duration, and intensity and specific work adjustment program needs. Since evaluating a person's stamina and tolerance for an eight-hour work day generally requires a long-term evaluation, resulting reports have the potential to address this often critical issue. Long-term assessments may allow for extensive career exploration and vocational awareness, which can be translated into client or student vocational decision-making. Ideally, long-term reports can present information on services and directions, which could result in the highest possible level of job placement available to the individual being evaluated.

Traditional Vocational Evaluations - These evaluations have historically been conducted by units housed in sheltered workshops, rehabilitation facilities, hospitals, and institutions that primarily receive referrals from, or make referrals to, rehabilitation counselors employed with state and federally funded vocational rehabilitation agencies. Depending on the length of the evaluation and the setting (i.e., vocational rehabilitation agency unit office, sheltered workshop, rehabilitation facility), the report goals identified above under the short-term and long-term evaluation sections will be appropriately addressed. Evaluation units in many state agency offices are often geared to providing short-term assessments to aid in eligibility determination and initial development of the Individualized Written Rehabilitation Program (IWRP). One critical recommendation often resulting from a short-term vocational evaluation is the need for an additional assessment of problems and needs that could not be adequately examined within a limited time frame.

In this situation, the long-term evaluations typically found in sheltered workshops and rehabilitation facilities are conducted. Recommendations may direct further service provision within that workshop or facility, such as work adjustment or remediation. Long-range IWRP planning and development guided by highly prescriptive recommendations is the focus of many traditional long-term evaluation reports.

To illustrate the difference that evaluation setting and length can make on the types of recommendations presented in a report, results from the previously cited vocational evaluation study conducted by the North Carolina Division of Vocational Rehabilitation Services (NCDVRS, 1983) will be enlisted. Three traditional vocational evaluation settings (sources) were incorporated into the study: a one-half day vocational evaluation provided by NCDVRS unit offices (ECSC), a several-day vocational evaluation conducted within hospital-based rehabilitation centers (RRC), and long-term sheltered workshop evaluations (SW). The top five recommendations are listed by the frequency with which they appeared in all 86 vocational evaluation reports analyzed. Note the differences, by priority, in the types of recommendations made.

RECOMMENDATIONS BY SOURCE
With Percent of Times Recommended

	ECSC	%	RRC	%	SW	%
1.	Job Placement (Direct, OJT)	37.5%	Counseling/Therapy	50%	Personnel/Social/Work Adjustment	69.4%
2.	Training (Vocational Skill)	35%	Job Placement (Selective)	30%	Job-Seeking Skills	30.6%
3.	Counseling/Therapy	32.5%	Remedial Education	20%	Job Placement (Direct, OJT)	30.6%
4.	Job Placement (Selective)	30%	GED	20%	Job Placement (Selective)	25%
5.	Higher Education (Community College, etc.)	22.5%	Job Placement (Direct)	20%	Counseling/Therapy	22.2%

Although these results could be attributed to sampling bias, a review of referral questions revealed a number of important facts that may also account for the pattern in the above recommendations by source. For example, it was found that clients were often referred to a sheltered workshop for an evaluation to determine if the additional services offered within that setting, such as work adjustment, would be of benefit to the individual in question. Further, clients may also have been sent to facilities that were specifically equipped to serve the particular needs of that individual. For example, mentally retarded individuals may have been referred to a sheltered workshop that primarily serves mentally retarded clients; physically disabled clients may be referred to a rehabilitation center that specializes in such conditions. This process of specializing in and providing services to specific client populations can result in an increased number of referrals in that area. In such a case, the types of referral questions and resulting report recommendations will typically address the specific evaluation needs of that group. Likewise, failure to meet the assessment needs of a particular population may result in diminished referrals.

School-Based Assessments - The primary objective of these evaluations is to "establish vocational goals for the Individualized Education Program (IEP)" (Ballantyne, 1985, p. 20; McCray, 1982). It is important to remember that vocational assessment can occur one or more times (depending on each student's needs) between the seventh grade and graduation, as well as in vocational schools and community colleges. Evaluations conducted at each grade level vary by student progress and by program and curriculum availability. Assessments conducted in the lower grades may focus more on curriculum needs, course placement, and instructional modification. Again, in the lower grades, pre-vocational (as opposed to vocational) issues may be of primary concern in the formulation of a comprehensive career development plan. Instructionally relevant assessment results could present options for appropriate classroom placement, optional teaching techniques, remedial needs, basic vocational interest and aptitude, curriculum development and modification, career education and hands-on exploratory activities, and functional living skills needs (Peterson, 1985).

As a student progresses into higher grades, assessments, as well as curriculum goals, expand. More specific and stable assessments of interest, vocational strengths and weaknesses, career counseling needs, present job-seeking and job-survival skills, specific equipment needs and modification, special program needs, and further education and training are included in the evaluation process (Special Programs Unit, 1985). Determining appropriate work experience program placements within the community or exploratory vocational course tryouts within the school may take priority in some assessment reports. Further assessments, over and above the lower grade evaluation, may be conducted to monitor student progress and to guide any need changes or updates in the student's IEP.

Evaluations offered prior to graduation may be used to identify and recommend vocational rehabilitation service needs, other community-based programs of services and support, additional education beyond the secondary school setting (e.g., trade, vocational, technical schools and courses, and apprenticeship programs), and job placement options such as on-the-job training, direct or selective placement, prescriptive job modification needs or supported work (Special Programs Unit, 1985). Depending on time lines and program or service availability, the types of assessments and resulting recommendations may vary by grade. Addressing needs to help students in their transition from school to work is the key to an effective assessment report in secondary school settings.

Evaluation conducted in post secondary school settings, such as technical schools and community colleges, may attempt to identify the most appropriate method of learning for the student, remedial academic needs, occupational interest and directions for exploration, and priority placements in vocational training programs. Previously underserved populations can be guided into the most appropriate training areas as long as report recommendations are related to the specific curriculums available through the institution.

Private-for-Profit Evaluations - The objectives of evaluation reports in proprietary settings depend primarily on the orientation of the evaluation. Whether adversarial or nonadversarial, these evaluations and resulting reports often tend to support a particular premise. When evaluating an injured worker in an industrial or personal injury case or an individual who has suffered due to product liability, final reports might address the individual's present or projected loss of earning capacity. Evaluations requested by insurance carriers and third parties might focus on rehabilitation potential and the feasibility of returning the individual to work. Reports written for social security disability determination cases frequently relate their findings to transferability of skills assessment. Other issues that might be emphasized in vocational reports relate to pre-injury versus post-injury condition, labor market survey results, part-time versus full-time employment potential (i.e., work stamina), level of work activity and tolerance of pain (frequency, duration, and intensity of activity and of the pain in question), and the probabilities of success in employment and training.

There are three basic types of vocational evaluation reports written in the proprietary sector; and they are the "feasibility evaluation" report, the "rehabilitation and placement" report, and the "forensic" report. "Feasibility" evaluations are generally administered as soon after injury as possible and are brief assessments designed to determine if the injured worker possesses any potential for rehabilitation services that would render him or her employable. In evaluating and identifying feasibility, Matheson (1984) recommends that "the patient as a worker must meet the general requirements an employer has of an employee" (p. 18). The three major feasibility categories that Matheson feels the injured worker must meet are: acceptable productivity (including quality), safety (to minimize further injury), and appropriate interpersonal behavior.

The "rehabilitation and placement" evaluation is a more comprehensive assessment, usually administered after the injured worker's medical condition has stabilized. This evaluation, similar to other evaluations, identifies and recommends specific rehabilitation, training, and job placement options. The "forensic" vocational evaluation and report may be used primarily in obtaining the best financial settlement possible for the party you are representing.

Regardless of the type of proprietary report being written, there is an important hierarchy of specific recommendations that Sink and King (1983) feel must be addressed by the evaluator:

1. The client can return to work in the same job with the same employer without modifications.

2. The client can return to work in the same job with the same employer with modifications.

3. The client can return to work with the same employer on a different job without modifications and at equal or better pay.

4. The client can return to work with the same employer on a

different job without modification at equal or better pay.

5. The client can return to work with a different employer at the same job without modification at equal or better pay.

6. The client can return to work with a different employer at the same job with modification at equal or better pay.

7. The client can return to work for a different employer on a job in which she or he has never been employed, but for which he or she has transferable skills and formal training is not required.

8. The client may return to work only if formal training is the only feasible alternative available and the client has the ability to successfully complete the training.

9. The client does not have potential for competitive employment. (p. 97)

Rehabilitation Coordinators, Incorporated (1981), identified five potential problem areas that might contribute to client failure:

A. <u>Physical</u> - What steps must be taken to promote healing and minimize permanency?

B. <u>Emotional</u> - What emotional problems serve as disincentives to return to work?

C. <u>Financial</u> - Do income benefits outweigh post-injury expenses? Is this a disincentive?

D. <u>Vocational</u> - Does patient have a vocational future?

<u>Motivational</u> - How have first four problem areas affected patient's motivation? (p. 1)

Vocational evaluators should always critically consider these five areas when conducting assessments, interpreting results, and writing reports. The placement alternatives hierarchy also used by Rehabilitation Coordinators, Incorporated, is very similar to that recommended by Sink and King, which is as follows:

A. Same Employer - Same Job
B. Same Employer - New/Modified Job
C. New Employer - Same/Similar Job
D. New Employer - New Job
E. Self-Employment/Additional Education. (p. 2)

The recommendation guidelines highlighted above present the most cost-effective placements first and progress to those options that take more time and money, and may demonstrate less likelihood for success. Deutsch and Sawyer (1985) very succinctly state the goals of this type of private-for-profit evaluation and its resulting report:

It is important for the client and the rehabilitation professional, as well as all other third parties involved, to understand that the rehabilitation evaluation always has a twofold purpose. First, the areas of damage vocationally, and the value (economically) of such damages, must be determined. Second, and of equal importance, a realistic plan to return the client to his or her maximum potential should be developed. (pp. 2-4)

One final market for proprietary vocational evaluations relates to identifying vocational options and new career directions for: displaced homemakers (e.g., widows and divorcees), displaced workers layed off due to technology or economics, underemployed or burned-out workers, individuals (e.g., housewives and graduates) who will be entering the labor market for the first time, and previously retired workers looking for new employment. This also includes evaluations contracted with business and industry for purposes of employment screening of applicants, and prioritizing existing employees for promotion, transfer, and additional training. These varied settings may require the development of highly specialized reports that are designed to answer unique and novel questions. In some cases, only a very brief report that answers a specific referral question will be required. In group screening situations, all applicants can be prioritized and discussed in the same report. In other cases, only a simple profile of evaluation results and/or a specific listing of potential or available jobs will need to be shared with the evaluee. These results would more than likely be accompanied by explanations and discussions of results and related vocational or training options, or extensive vocational counseling, as new vocational assessment markets surface, so will the potential for variations in reporting the results.

Conclusion

Evaluation length, type, and setting all have a direct effect on the overall content and outcome of a vocational evaluation and assessment report. In spite of these differences, report results should ultimately relate to employment. Without a vocational orientation, what evaluators do is hard to define, thus diminishing their potential value and impact. Although cross-setting evaluations can be successfully conducted, their appropriateness to the user will only be assured when the resulting reports specifically tie outcomes to programs, services, and jobs that are available to that particular user. Succinctly expressed, evaluation setting and orientation have a direct impact on report content, length, and use.

Chapter VI

DEVELOPING REPORT OUTCOME OPTIONS

Defining Evaluation and Assessment by Outcome

As mentioned in the previous chapter, the ultimate outcome of a vocational evaluation report is to recommend vocational programs and options that eventually lead to employment. Since we can define assessment primarily by what we say in a report, we should be fully aware of our limits (i.e., what we can document and prove, what we can legally say, what can be realistically recommended based on availability). This focus on the real rather than the ideal makes our report a living document whose value can only be measured by its usefulness to the referral source. The previous chapter addressed the issues of writing in different settings. This chapter details a wide range of recommendations that are made regardless of setting. Although identifying job placement possibilities is the primary objective of the writer, and is given top billing in the following list, the remaining recommendation options are by no means in descending order of importance, other than the fact that they are necessary to supporting and enhancing employment potential.

1. Direct Job Placement - This refers to making recommendations for jobs that the student or client is immediately prepared to enter. As a rule, when direct placement recommendations are made, it is felt that the evaluee has the potential to seek out and interview for that job (or jobs) and competitively perform it without any placement or on-the-job assistance. Self-employment should also be included in this category unless there are selective or prescriptive needs, in which case they will be placed under one of the next two categories.

2. Selective Job Placement - Jobs in this category are chosen because they can potentially be performed by the client under certain conditions, in spite of existing problems and limitations. For example: due to poor grooming, a client is placed on a job where such problems can be overlooked (heavy construction, grounds maintenance); individuals who cannot read are placed on jobs where reading is not required; a student who does not get along well with other people is recommended for employment where he/she can work alone; a patient who does not deal well with stress is found a stress-free environment; and someone who cannot get to work on time in the morning is recommended for jobs that begin later in the day. In many instances, some assistance with finding, learning, and keeping jobs (e.g., job coaching) may be necessary and should be explained in the recommendation.

3. Prescriptive Job Placement - Recommendations for this highly conditional type of employment require that certain contingencies be met before any kind of placement can be initiated. Not only do selective conditions and environments (as discussed in #2 above) need to be considered, but job accommodations will also be required. This complex placement process may be the only available option for some severely disabled individuals. For example, a stress-free, low-paced, sedentary work environment may need to be found in which visually oriented instruction with extended periods of practice and long-term job coaching can be offered. Rehabilitation engineering may be frequently prescribed as the only way to effect a specific kind of job placement.

4. <u>On-the-Job Training</u> - Recommendations in this category relate to jobs that provide specific training at the time of employment. As with other areas of education and training, instructional modifications may be outlined that could improve overall job learning and performance for clients with special problems. For many individuals, recommendations for work experience placements or subcontract work area placements may be an important first step to on-the-job training.

5. <u>Remedial Education</u> - Often, pre-employment improvements in academic, independent living, or functional working areas are necessary. For example, a single skill such as reading may need improvement before vocational or independent living training and placement can realistically occur. Client success in taking and passing the GED may require specialized preparation through remediation. For individuals who have barriers to learning, prescriptive recommendations for instructional and curriculum modifications can be presented.

6. <u>Technical, Vocational, or Apprenticeship Training</u> - Such training is more job-oriented rather than academically oriented. It may lead to the attainment of a degree, diploma, or certificate indicating a certain level of attainment or expertise in a skilled area. Prescriptions for instructional or curriculum modifications may be essential to improved learning and performance.

7. <u>Formal Education</u> - Courses and curriculum leading to academic attainment, a high school diploma, or a degree from a community college or university would be recommended in this category. Courses may relate to college preparation, a liberal arts curriculum, or to professional development. Prescriptive recommendations for instructional and curriculum modifications may be necessary to overcome specific learning problems.

8. <u>Job Readiness Training</u> - Job-seeking and/or job-survival skills training may be important recommendations to assist clients in finding and keeping employment. Job-seeking skills are those essential abilities needed to correctly locate and apply for jobs and effectively interview for them. Job-survival skills are those attributes that make good employees: good attendance, appropriate grooming and dress, getting along with supervisors and co-workers, and correctly following rules and regulations. Clients who possess good job-seeking and job-survival skills can usually be recommended for direct placement. Those who do not may need work adjustment services or selective or prescriptive placement (i.e., job-placement assistance, job coaching). Particular job-seeking and job-survival needs should also be spelled out in this type of recommendation.

9. <u>Adjustment Services (Work, Personal, Social)</u> - Clients falling into this recommendation category often have significant barriers to employment and independent living that restrict successful functioning. Rather than recommending specific types of adjustment techniques that should be used, providing descriptive detail on the frequency, duration, and magnitude (or severity) of the problem behavior in question would be more beneficial to the referral source and adjustment personnel.

10. <u>Counseling or Therapy</u> - When a recommendation for these services is made, documenting the problem and justifying the particular reason counseling or therapy should be provided would help the referral source identify an appropriate counseling goal and strategy or therapist. If the problem is serious, then the evaluator may want to contact the referral source immediately so that the client

can receive prompt attention, rather than waiting until the report has been received and the recommendation read and acted upon much later.

11. Career Exploration - In cases where the evaluation process and client have been unable to target a specific occupational interest, career exploration and related activities and services should be recommended to assist the individual with vocational awareness and decision making.

12. Independent Living Needs - Recommendations for the acquisition of transportation, activities of daily living skills, and recreational activities and programs may be essential to finding and maintaining stable employment. In some instances, identifying the most appropriate living environment (e.g., group home, halfway house, modified house or apartment, or other sheltered or accommodated community living arrangement) may need to accompany job-related recommendations.

13. Rehabilitation Engineering - Technological advances have opened new doors in employment, training, education, and independent living for citizens with disabilities. Although evaluators may not be able to keep track of the many new and continuing developments, general recommendations for accommodation, modification, and rehabilitation engineering should be made whenever possible. More importantly, recommending consultation with various research facilities, companies, or individuals that specialize in rehabilitation engineering, adaptive equipment, or modified work and living environments gives referral agencies the resources to better serve their clients' total needs.

14. Sheltered Workshop Placement - At times, it is the opinion of the assessment specialist that the client, patient, or student could profit from work hardening, work adjustment, or related services in order to improve the individual's work quality, quantity, stamina, and job-related behavior. Therefore, referral to a transitional facility that provides: (a) a paid work experience commensurate with the individual's level of productivity, (b) latitude for variations in performance and behavior, and (c) a controlled environment in which to conduct work adjustment should be considered. Referrals can also be made to hospitals and private-for-profit companies that offer effective work-hardening services but may not provide a "paid" work experience. Workshop and work-hardening recommendations should also indicate why such a referral is being made and what kinds of services are needed to improve the clients chances for employment.

15. Sheltered Employment - There are a few individuals whose work capacity, although consistent, is generally in the borderline competitive range or whose behavior, disability, or handicap greatly restricts their employability. These individuals may find themselves most appropriately placed in permanent sheltered employment positions in work centers or sheltered workshops. Depending on their orientation, supported work positions or work enclaves within business and industry could provide individuals with a protected long-term work environment or an opportunity for transition into competitive employment, once the job requirements have been reached.

16. Return to the Referral Source for Further Evaluation - A need for additional vocational, educational, physical, sensory, medical, psychological, or mental evaluations may be documented, justified, and recommended when vocational evaluation specialists feel that further information is needed before a vocational recommendation can be followed or

even rendered. Prosthetic evaluations, specialist reviews, physical capacity evaluations, personality assessments, neuro-psychological evaluations, or screenings of vision, hearing, and speech are a few of the additional types of evaluative and diagnostic services to which vocational evaluators may refer to their reports.

17. <u>Eligibility Determination</u> - This broad spectrum of recommendations may assist any number of agencies in determining their client's or student's eligibility to receive various kinds of benefits or services, qualify for and enter various programs, or receive numerous forms of assistance. More specifically, reports may be used in part, but not limited to, determining eligibility for: vocational rehabilitation or rehabilitation facility services; admission into various school programs, courses, or curriculums; appropriate correctional program placement; and receiving social security and other forms of disability payments. However, this may be one of many reports (e.g., medical, psychological) that would be used in determining eligibility.

A broader aspect of eligibility determination in the private-for-profit sector relates to the initial evaluation of an injured worker's ability to return to work following vocational rehabilitation services. If the return-to-work probability is low, then a determination of the client's loss of earning capacity would be in order. From a legal standpoint, the individual's potential for rehabilitation and subsequent employment and his/her eligibility for the receipt of disabled worker compensation and benefits must be accurately determined for purposes of final settlement.

18. <u>Closure</u> - When an individuals' work capacity is found to be inconsequential, even with the provision of extensive habilitation and rehabilitation programming, then vocational rehabilitation services will generally be discontinued. However, instead of matter-of-factly recommending that an individual be closed out as infeasible, the vocational evaluator should:

(a) document and justify why closure is being recommended;
(b) refer the evaluee to other beneficial programs, services, or activities;
(c) indicate why these programs, services, or activities are being recommended and what they would accomplish; and
(d) offer to re-evaluate the individual if, at a later date, there is a change in his/her status.

Examples of other programs, services, or activities would be to refer your client for mental health or mental retardation services, substance abuse services, and work activities or adult day-care center placement.

Functional Outcomes: Selected Studies of Report Recommendations

The Vocational Evaluation and Work Adjustment Association (Pell, Fry, and Langton, 1983) defines <u>functional outcomes</u> as "Activities in which a person is capable of engaging on a regular basis and which require the use of time, strength, or faculties" (p. 5). All functional activities identified by VEWAA have some economic value, and those functions relating to gainful employment head the list. VEWAA's (1975) <u>Vocational Evaluation Project Final Report</u> presented results from a study that illustrates the types of functional outcome recommendations given in vocational evaluation reports. The study identifies a wide range of recommendations typically valued by manpower service agencies. It is interesting to note that gainful employment was <u>not</u> recommended for slightly more than one-fifth of the evaluees included in the following results.

Recommended Optimal Functional Outcomes for
Vocational Evaluation Service Recipients

Functional Outcome	%
COMPETITIVE EMPLOYMENT	57.6
Self-employed	0.9
Career	15.3
Long-term	11.7
Short-term	9.0
Marginal	17.1
Sub-productive	3.6
SHELTERED EMPLOYMENT	17.1
Transitional	6.3
Long-term	10.8
HOMEBOUND EMPLOYMENT	1.8
Self-employed	0.9
Employee	0.9
OTHER	21.6
Work activities programming - long-term	2.7
Volunteer work	0.0
Unpaid home work - care of home and other family members	0.0
Community activity - individual use of time	0.9
Programmed day activities	0.0
Homebound - individual use of time in home	0.0
Homebound - independent total self-care	0.9
Family/community assistance - partial self-care	2.7
Structured living environment - partial self-care	0.9
Total dependence on others - short-term	3.6
Total dependence on others - long-term	7.2
Not determined	2.7

*Listing adapted from Morris, R. Welfare Reform 1973: The social services dimension. Science, 1973, 181, 515-522. (VEWAA, 1975, p. 28)

Another report recommendation study was conducted by the North Carolina Department of Vocational Rehabilitation Services (NCDVRS, 1983). This previously cited research analyzed and categorized recommendations contained in 86 randomly selected vocational evaluation reports generated in three different rehabilitation settings (vocational rehabilitation unit offices, rehabilitation hospitals, and sheltered workshops). An average of 2.7 recommendations was made for each evaluee from the following table:

Rank Ordered Frequency of
Recommended Activity - All VE Sources Combined

Activity Recommended	Responses	%
Personal/Social/Work Adjustment	34	14.8
Job Placement (Direct, OJT)	28	12.2
Counseling/Therapy	26	11.3
Job Placement (Selective)	24	10.4
Further Services (e.g., evaluation, prosthetics, medical)	21	9.1
Training (Vocational Skill)	20	8.7
Remedial Education (e.g., reading, writing, spelling...)	18	7.8
Job-Seeking Skills	15	6.5
GED	12	5.2
Career Exploration	11	4.8
Higher Education (Community College, etc.)	11	4.8
Sheltered Employment (Workshop)	7	3.0
Independent Living (ADL, communications, transportation, etc.)	3	1.3

(NCDVRS, 1983, Addendum)

The increasing emphasis on transitional services, supported employment, and work stations in industry has created a unique approach to job training and placement. These approaches can be translated into a hierarchy of long-term and short-term recommendations. Hagner and Como (1982) discussed such employment and training options as a continuum from dependent to independent, that "...can either extend or largely replace a traditional sheltered workshop" (p. 3). They also refer to the work of DuRand and Neufeld (1980) in which work stations in industry are considered to be a bridge between sheltered workshops and competitive employment. When considering the range of possible recommendations in this area, the following list should give the evaluator important direction.

1. Sheltered Employment: All handicapped work force. Largely subsidized.

2. Sheltered Industry: Largely handicapped work force with non-handicapped worker models. May be partly subsidized.

3. Semi-Sheltered Employment (Group): Non-handicapped work force with groups of handicapped. Regular industry.

4. Competitive Work With Support: Non-handicapped work force with individual handicapped persons with support. Regular industry.

5. Individual Competitive Employment: Regular work hours. All workers trained equally. Regular industry. (Hagner and Como, p.3)

Recommendations derived from this list can be used individually or in combination to help the worker reach any targeted level of employment.

The Recommendation Checklist

To assist the evaluator with formulating report recommendations on each client, a standard recommendation checklist should be developed. Begin by identifying general recommendations you are capable of making based on your type of evaluation, availability of jobs and services, and needs of your clients and referral sources. Organize a brief checklist with recommendation categories similar to those listed at the beginning of this chapter, allowing space for descriptive and prescriptive statements. When it is time to write a report, simply develop your report outline and complete the recommendation checklist. Choose those recommendations most appropriate for the client, add necessary comments in the space provided, and prioritize your recommendations in the order they will be listed in the report. This is an excellent method for organizing your thoughts and ensuring that nothing is overlooked or left out.

A brief example of such a checklist is as follows:

RECOMMENDATION CHECKLIST

_____ Placement (direct/selective/prescriptive)
1.
2.
3.

_____ Training (OJT/formal/remedial)
1.
2.
3.

_____ Adjustment Services (work/personal/social)

_____ Counseling/Therapy (state reasons)

_____ Sheltered Employment (type/setting)

_____ Other Services (specify)

Conclusion

In essence, vocational evaluation is defined by what can be recommended for an individual in his/her final report. Although reports should primarily focus on identifying gainful employment options, they should also list and explain any services that would help develop or further enhance employability. In many instances, and particularly with individuals severely disabled or requiring multiple services, numerous recommendations may be necessary in helping the person achieve independence. The type of recommendations being made, and their priority, will depend primarily on client/student needs and orientation of the referral source.

Chapter VII

TYPES OF EVALUATION AND ASSESSMENT REPORTS

Choosing a Report Type

There is a wide variety of report types and styles available to the vocational evaluator. Although the narrative report is the most frequently "written" type of report, it is not always the "preferred" type by either the author or the user. They are generally the longer and more difficult ones to prepare and, on occasion, the lengthier and more complex ones for the referral source to read and use. However, many evaluators prefer to stick with one type as opposed to jumping from one style to another. What an evaluator chooses to use often hinges on four considerations.

1. Writing and Evaluation Skill - Individuals who are new to assessment and the unique form of report writing that it demands may be far more comfortable using checklists, checklist combinations (narrative/checklist), brief one-page summary reports, or computer-generated reports. Evaluators who have difficulty writing may prefer checklists, checklist combinations, or computer-generated reports.

2. Evaluation Length and Client Load - Short evaluations and screenings, and those that have limited report turnaround time, may dictate a need for computer-generated, checklist, checklist combination, or summary reports. Longer evaluations, small caseloads, and liberal turnaround time may lend themselves better to narrative reports.

3. Clerical Support - Evaluators who have access to clerical staff for typing reports can be highly flexible in the report style they choose. However, when this support is lacking, then the use of extensive narrative formats will more than likely be limited as well.

4. Needs of the Referral Source - If referral agents are only looking for brief or specific kinds of information (e.g., job possibilities, program, or service options), then comprehensive narrative reports may not be necessary. Since identifying employment directions should be the focal point of evaluation reports, they should be geared to identifying as many feasible jobs as possible. The report is the final product of evaluation, and the most important document that is purchased by the referral source. With this in mind, writers must insure that their reports provide the purchaser with sufficient job-related information if they plan to continue marketing these same products in the future.

The remainder of this chapter will be devoted to describing four types of reports: narrative, checklist, combination narrative checklist, and computer generated. Although this publication will focus on the narrative report, this in no way means that, when used appropriately, other report types have less value. In fact, evaluators who conduct assessments for a wide range of referral sources may use a variety of report types, depending on the four considerations listed above.

The Narrative Report

As previously mentioned, the narrative is the most common type of report (Esser, 1974). It allows the author to personalize information and explain subtle, yet pertinent, detail. It is generally divided into three sections: demographic/biographic/identifying information; the body of the report, which documents and justifies the interpretations and outcomes; and the summary and recommendations. Many narrative reports will typically exceed three pages and may contain additional appendices or addendums supporting the narrative and helping to keep it concise. These types of narrative reports are the most comprehensive and detailed and can specifically guide the planning process. At the same time, they may also be too lengthy and complex for the user to easily distill pertinent facts that are critical to efficient service provision.

However, in some instances, a brief one- or two-page summary report may be all the narrative that is needed by the referral source. In any event, the narrative report is the most flexible, allowing for variation and tailoring of the content and descriptions, depending on what is most important to the client and referral agent. Unfortunately, these report types are the most complicated to prepare and consequently take the most time. This may create problems with contradictions, double meanings, confusion, and overall report continuity. They also take the greatest length of time to learn how to write correctly.

The Checklist Report

This type of report, also known as the basic checklist (Esser, 1974), is the quickest and simplest report to prepare. It is often used in highly production oriented evaluation units and by evaluators with limited report writing skills. There are three general types of checklist reports:

1. Discrete checklists - These forced choice checklists require the rater to make separate, or even dichotomous choices (e.g., yes/no, acceptable/unacceptable, competitive/non-competitive, above average/average/below average, good/fair/poor) as they relate to behavioral and performance statements. Likert-type scales are often used in this kind of checklist. In other cases, discrete checklists may require the rater to check only those statements, numerical or verbal, which apply to the client (e.g., top 10%, easily distracted, cooperative). There can be no "in between" rating as there is with a continuous checklist.

2. Continuous checklists - Using horizontal or vertical rating scales, ratings are based on a continuous measure. Using discrete statements (e.g., below average, average, above average), which are placed equidistant along a continuous line, or dichotomous statements (e.g., below average, above average) placed on either end of a line, evaluators can mark anywhere on the line between two statements to convey a subtle difference that cannot be delineated by a discrete rating.

3. Descriptive checklists - Behavior and performance are depicted through descriptive words (e.g., adjectives), phrases, or statements. By choosing words or phrases that best typify the individual's functioning, the reader can visualize the student or client in ways that cannot be conveyed by purely discrete or continuous ratings.

Various combinations of these three types of checklist reports can be incorporated to provide the most accurate picture possible of the evaluee. Unfortunately, checklists do not give the reader much descriptive detail, insight, or understanding into the why's and how's of a person's problems, behaviors, or functioning. They do, however, provide good interpretive information and an excellent outline for narrative report writing. Checklists are also highly amenable to computerization.

The Narrative Checklist

This incorporates the first two report types that were previously discussed (Esser, 1974). There are two different formats for the combination narrative checklist. The first format calls for two separate documents, the checklist and the narrative report. In this situation, the checklist is either used as an appendix to the narrative report or the narrative report is appended at the end of the checklist. One document clarifies the other. When developed separately, the checklist can be used as a report writing outline for the narrative and included at the beginning or end of the final report.

The second format intertwines the checklist and narrative into one single document. Each discrete or continuous item is immediately followed by a brief narrative statement, in sentence or phrase form, which documents and justifies the rating. This allows for an explanation of each rating, which is not given in the pure checklist report type. For example, if a client's grooming was below average on the first day but above average on the second, how would you rate the grooming item on a pure checklist report? However, the combination narrative checklist allows readers to quickly review or skim the ratings to obtain a general picture of the evaluee, and at the same time provides brief but pertinent facts concerning the more critical ratings.

These combination reports often lack the continuity found in a narrative report. It is also difficult to show interaction between various behaviors and situations. Secondly, combination reports may not be the best vehicle for explaining individual test and work sample results, unless the checklist and narrative are developed as two separate documents, or appropriately appended.

Computer-Generated Reports

This is the newest of the report types and has only recently surfaced with the advent of the micro or personal computer. However, these report formats were first popularized through computer scoring, interpreting, and report writing services that were dedicated to main frame computers. Computer scoring services for personality, intelligence, and interest testing initially capitalized on this concept. Main frame computers could be accessed either by mailing in the answer sheets for computer scoring or by entering the data on a terminal that was connected by a special telephone hookup to the main frame. Two of the first commercially marketed work sample systems to take advantage of this main frame technology were the Comprehensive Occupational Assessment and Training System (COATS) and the Career Evaluation Systems (Botterbusch, 1982). Today, many of the commercially marketed vocational assessment systems offer computerized scoring, job matching, and report preparation. There are two types of computer-generated reports: word processed and system dedicated.

Word processed evaluation reports come in several varieties. The first are reports composed using readily available word processing software. These software packages allow evaluators or clerical staff to prepare assessment reports and other documents (e.g., letters, contracts, forms) on a personal computer. They also permit the user to develop a standard report format and a file of common statements (e.g., test, work sample, and norm group descriptions) that can be repeatedly used on command to reduce writing and typing time. The second variety are those customized word processing packages that are specifically designed for writing vocational evaluation and general rehabilitation reports (Shainline, 1984). They can be purchased from psychological tests, rehabilitation, and human service software marketers, and already contain files of standardized formats for writing up intake and interview reports, functional assessment outcomes, and a variety of test and work sample descriptions and results. These packages have diverse applications in assessment, and the software menu generally contains a variety of instrument write-ups to choose from. In many instances, any number of instruments and techniques can be used with the software.

System dedicated evaluation reports are generated from software that has been developed for use with a particular test or work sample system. Report writing software that has been developed for a specific work sample system can only be used with that system. For example, software used to prepare reports for the Microcomputer Evaluation and Screening Assessment (MESA) system developed by the VALPAR International Corporation cannot be used to score and interpret client results from the APTICOM developed by the Vocational Research Institute, and vice versa (Harris, 1982; Vocational Evaluation and Work Adjustment Association, 1984). Although dedicated packages are limited in their use to a single work sample system, they can reduce report writing time dramatically when evaluations are confined to that one system. An inherent problem of such swift computer-generated reports is the possible complacency created in evaluators who rely solely on the computer for report writing, to the extent that they feel the report does not need to be proofed for accuracy. With regard to comprehensive system dedicated software, which scores, interprets, writes reports, and conducts job matches, Matarazzo (1983) in his editorial "Computerized Psychological Testing" states that:

> It is critically important that the legions of users of such automated tests be reminded forth-rightly that the predictive value of the test, technically called their validity, remains to be scientifically appraised. To date, there is no evidence published in peer-reviewed journals that one full page of the narrative descriptions is valid. (Editorial)

Until a user is confident that such comprehensive system dedicated reports are accurate and representative of both the evaluee's functioning and the current labor market, then these reports should be used with caution, supplemented with descriptive and interpretive comments or attachments, or used as a guideline in conducting further assessment and report writing. Lastly, without the addition of comments in a computer-generated report, they will tend to read very much like a fill-in-the-blank report.

Report Packages

When a wide range of evaluation services is offered to a client on a team approach (e.g., social, sensory, psychological, educational, physical, vocational) within one facility, all final results can be combined into one report, or prepared as separate documents and organized into a report package. This would prevent confusion for the referral source that is created by mailing out a variety of separate reports on the same client at different times, which eliminates any continuity in information gathering and planning. When results from different disciplines are combined into one report, each section within the report could be devoted to a separate specialty area. The summary and recommendations section could then incorporate and interpret the results from each area, with the goal of explaining or eliminating any contradictions and increasing overall report utility (VALPAR-SPECTIVE, 1975).

On the other hand, report packages may be used when the various reports are either too long or too diverse to combine into a single report. This may call for organizing the separate reports in some kind of order (e.g., chronologically), beginning with a table of contents and possibly concluding with a summary statement and recommendations. Whether it is decided to incorporate the results of all disciplines into one report or to include them in a package of separate reports, the organizer may want to place the summary and recommendations section in the very beginning to serve as an abstract for the reader.

The remaining chapters in this book will focus on narrative report writing. Since this is one of the most frequently used and most difficult forms of report preparation, it will receive the greatest attention.

Conclusion

There are four basic types of vocational evaluation and assessment reports: narrative, checklist, combination narrative checklist, and computer generated. Although the narrative report is the most frequently prepared, what an evaluator chooses as a format depends to a great extent on writing and evaluation skill, evaluation length and client load, clerical support, and needs of the referral source. Comprehensive evaluations conducted as a team in large facilities may require the use of a report package to coordinate all findings into a cohesive plan of action.

Chapter VIII

PREPARING TO WRITE A REPORT

Organizing the File

Once an evaluee has exited the process, the assessment specialist should first make sure that all pertinent data (e.g., referral information, interview and behavior observation forms, score sheets) are in the working file. The file should then be arranged in chronological order; that is, the order in which information was obtained, starting with the referral information and intake interview and ending with the exit interview.

At this point, the file should be reviewed in order, one page at a time. During this analysis and synthesis stage, the evaluator is trying to determine if there are patterns of vocational behaviors and results. Interpretive notes could be taken to aid in determining if patterns do, in fact, exist and what it means to employability potential. The reviewer should also be very sensitive to how the results relate to the original referral question(s). By now, what the evaluator wants to say and how it will be organized and written up should start to take shape.

The file and resulting notes are then organized in such a way that they can be very effectively and efficiently shared in a final staffing. Results of the evaluation should be presented in the same way the report will be written, with emphasis placed on how the referral questions will be answered. Feedback from those attending the staffing will give final input and approval to what will be included in the report (i.e., the report becomes a synopsis of the staffing). When an evaluator can share with significant others what he or she plans to write in a report and receives input, support, and an endorsement for the final product, it gives the author greater confidence in what is being written. Furthermore, if the referral source and evaluee are in attendance and agree to the proposed plan of action, it ensures that the forthcoming report will be of use in the planning process.

It is recommended that if final staffings are used as part of the evaluation process, they be conducted <u>prior</u> to the writing of the final vocational assessment report. The experience of many evaluators has shown that, quite often, evaluation reports that are completed prior to the final staffing will, in one way or another, need to be amended. This wastes time and money needlessly generated in rewriting and retyping the original report or developing a supplemental one.

Organizing the Outline

Once the staffing is complete and the resulting notes are added at the end of the file, the process of outline development can begin. Although most evaluation units maintain a standard report writing outline, there may be a need to make subtle or even dramatic changes in how it will be written so that it can be tailored to a particular treatment of the final results and to the needs of the referral source. For instance, you may decide to write your report in the order in which information was obtained (chronological order), by best to worst performance, or grouped by type of instrument administered (interviews, psychometric tests, work samples, situational assessments). Once you have decided how to organize and write the report, arrange the information in your file in that order and modify or develop your report writing outline accordingly. The resulting outline, which is arranged in the same order as your file information, is now ready to be used as your report writing guide.

With the outline developed, start entering descriptive words or phrases at key points throughout the outline to serve as information prompts and file references during the writing process. This should help minimize redundancy and contradictions and reduce overall report length and writing time. For evaluators who decide to use a combination narrative checklist report, where both documents are developed separately, the checklist can serve as the report writing outline. By entering key words or phrases beside each rating on a working copy of the checklist, not only can they serve as a writing prompt but as a guide in how to justify the various ratings on the checklist. Such an outline or checklist is particularly critical when dictation equipment is used in report writing.

Tips on Using Dictation Equipment

Using dictation equipment to prepare a report is not only fast and efficient, but it may help to delay or minimize report writing burnout. Before an evaluator begins dictating a report, it is often recommended that he/she first become familiar with assessment reports by handwriting the first few and enlisting a colleague or supervisor to review and critique them. As the writing process becomes more familiar and comfortable, then dictation can be attempted. Many individuals are often reluctant to learn how to dictate reports due to their lack of familiarity with the equipment and the dictating process, and a feeling that their dictation will be imperfect. Reluctance also stems from poor organization of thoughts and materials (Popham, Tilton, Jackson, and Hanna, 1983), such as results and outcomes, file information, and the report writing outline.

1. Learn how to operate your dictation equipment. Thoroughly review any operations manuals. Become very familiar with the process of how to review and make corrections in your dictation. You may want to practice dictating a few report sections and then play them back to see if you can understand what was said. Evaluate your pronunciation, dictating speed, and instructions to the typist and make appropriate corrections. If you cannot distinguish what you are dictating, imagine the problems your typist will have. (Himstreet and Bay, 1984; Popham, et al., 1983).

2. Provide your typist with a sample report. In situations where your typist is not familiar with how a report is organized and spaced, provide a sample format that can be used as a guide. Other special instructions, such as sentence spacing, formatting, underlining, indenting, and the number of copies needed, can be routinely established when a sample report is given to the typist. This approach will eliminate the need to repeatedly give format instructions over the dictaphone every time you begin a report.

3. At the beginning of each dictation, indicate who you are, what you are about to dictate (e.g., vocational evaluation report, letter, memo), and any special instructions, such as spacing and number of copies (Himstreet and Bay, 1984).

4. Speak slowly and distinctly. Dictate with logical phrasing, pausing between thought groups. (Himstreet and Baty, 1984; Popham, et al., 1983).

5. Himstreet and Bay (1984, p. 126) state that, "In dictating initials, speak slowly and overemphasize

the pronunciation of the following letters: B, F, H, M, N, P, S, T, V, X, Z. In dictating ordinal numbers overemphasize the pronunciation of second, fifth, sixth, seventh, fifteenth, seventeenth. When unusual words or names are used, spell them. For example, Aaron and Erin are pronounced similarly. To use Erin, you should say, 'Erin, that's capital E-r-i-n.'

6. Indicate quotes, capital letters (first or all letters), commas, periods, dashes, and possessives (Mary's students') by dictating these instructions as they are needed (Himstreet and Baty, 1984).

7. Use rules of common etiquette. Do not make unnecessary noises while the dictating equipment is running. Turn it off, when you plan to clear your throat, cough, sneeze, laugh, yawn, talk with someone else, or when the telephone rings. Rather than saying "um" or "uh" or pausing for an excessive period of time while thinking of what it is you want to say, turn off the dictaphone until you are ready to speak. Do not tell jokes or make funny or unnecessary statements while dictating. Respect your typist.

8. Rather than spelling out technical or difficult words that you often use, provide your typist with a list of these words for reference purposes.

Once you have completed your first dictated report, play it back to see how you did. You may want to repeat this playback process for several reports if problems (e.g., repetitions, contradictions, poor dictation) are discovered. This feedback process allows for self-evaluation and focuses attention on specific areas for improvement.

After the dictated report has been typed, the evaluator should proof it. As with the playback process, problems with organization, wording, repetition, and contradictions need to be identified. Further, the accuracy of the data (e.g., ages, dates, scores) should be carefully examined. And lastly, check for correct spelling, capitalization, and use of punctuation.

Probably the best combination for fast, efficient report writing is the use of dictating equipment by the evaluator and word processing equipment by the typist. As long as a word processor is being used, liberal changes in report content can be made during the proofing process creating few, if any, problems for the typist during test revision and final typing. For the most part, the word processing hardware and software you choose is a matter of personal preference, but should be flexible enough to readily adapt to future changes in report format and style.

Conclusion

In preparing to write a report, the evaluator should start by organizing the working file in the order the report is to be written. This should be followed by the development of a new, or modification of an existing, report writing outline. Key words and phrases could be added at appropriate places throughout the outline to prompt the evaluator in what to write. If dictation equipment is used, then the evaluator should learn the proper procedure for dictating reports. The author needs to carefully proof the rough draft of every report before final typing. Use of a word processor by the typist would allow the evaluator freedom to make changes in report content while increasing the speed and efficiency with which reports are prepared.

Chapter IX

THE REPORT FORMAT

Components of a Report

As previously mentioned, report formats may vary for any number of reasons. Evaluation purposes, setting, process, length, outcomes, and, most importantly, referral questions will influence organization of the report format and content. As discussed in Chapter IV, report formats may be modified not only to meet the specific needs of different referral sources, but to minimize report writing burnout by varying the routine of writing. Regardless of the reasons for modification, vocational evaluation and assessment reports generally contain similar components and similar kinds of information (Esser, 1974). The manuals of most of the commercially available vocational evaluation systems recommend report writing formats that can be specifically used with each individual system (Botterbusch, 1982). The four components of a narrative evaluation or assessment report are:

1. Identifying information (biographic/demographic)
2. Body of the report (for documentation and justification)
3. Summary and recommendations
4. Report attachments (appendices)

The identifying information establishes the client identity; the body of the report explains what happened during the evaluation and interprets, documents, and justifies the results; the summary abstracts what was written in the body of the report, and the recommendations identify plans of action; and the report attachments provide additional information on test/work sample descriptions and outcomes. This would be a particularly effective arrangement in situations where individuals reading and using evaluation reports (e.g., school teachers) may not have a good understanding of vocational assessment or know what to expect from a report. Reading the summary and recommendations section first may give them a better appreciation for the documentation in the body of the report, and a clearer understanding of what was done, why it was done, and how it was used in formulating final decisions. In this case, the report becomes an effective orientation and public relations tool for the first-time reader. Smith (1971) identified three essential areas of information that should be contained in every evaluation report:

1. disability and limitations
2. client assets, and
3. alternative vocational plans (p. 192).

Based on the disability and limitations, and client assets information that has been gathered throughout the assessment process, the evaluator is able to develop alternative vocational plans; and in most cases, a report concludes with the summary and recommendations section. However, some writers have included the summary and recommendations at the beginning. Since it is the main feature of a report, it is, therefore, considered to be the first and foremost section that should be read.

Formats by Setting

To examine the wide range of possible report formats, we must again consider how such evaluation reports are organized for traditional rehabilitation, school, and private-for-profit settings. Further, we cannot overlook the writer's preference for a specific format that would best meet her or his particular style of writing. Esser (1974) presented a basic yet comprehensive format that stressed the information needs typical to vocational rehabilitation settings.

The organization and content of his topical outline, listed below, "...is primarily determined by the writer's judgment" (p. 11).

1) Identifying Information (e.g., client and evaluator's name, referral source, dates of evaluation and report, case and/or social security numbers, date of client's birth)

2) Reason for Referral

3) Background Information (e.g., disability, education, family environment, and work history pertinent to client's vocational problems and prognosis)

4) Psychological and Vocational Test Results

5) Work Performance

6) Work Habits and Behaviors

7) Physical Characteristics (e.g., ability to work an eight-hour day, vocational restrictions based on physical limitations)

8) Summary and Recommendations

   A. Vocational Assets

   B. Vocational Limitations

   C. Recommendations

      1. Immediate Objectives
      2. Long-term Objectives

   D. Summary Statement (pp. 12-15)

Report formats in educational settings have some unique differences from Esser's topical outline. The Occupational Curriculum Laboratory (1982) presented the "Basic Vocational Assessment Report," which is written prior to offering a comprehensive vocational assessment. Their outline, given below, stresses student placement within school vocational programs.

1) Student Information (e.g., name, grade, handicap, present program placement, date)

2) Vocational Assessment Questions

3) Special Education Test Data (e.g., Diagnostician, test, results, date, comments)

4) Student Interview (e.g., interviewer, date, interests, career awareness, family support, comments)

5) Parent Interview (e.g., interviewer, date, career plans for student, support for working, comments)

6) Information Gathered During Instruction (source, skills and needs for mental abilities, functional academic skills, sensory abilities, learning style, functional life skills, vocational interests, prevocational skills, work attitude and behavior)

7) Aptitude and Interest (e.g., administrator, location, date, results, interpretation, and comments)

8) Answers to Assessment Questions

9) Recommendations (e.g., need and reason for a comprehensive vocational assessment, vocational program/placement, functional life skills, and related academics) (pp. 111-113)

A more comprehensive, school-based, vocational evaluation report format was developed by the New Jersey State Department of Education (1978) and is as follows:

1) Introduction (e.g., attendance, social interaction/interaction

with peers, interaction with evaluator)

2) Career Goals (e.g., interests, realistic or unrealistic)

3) Work Samples/On-the-Job Evaluation/Psychometrics (e.g., performance, work habits, level of frustration, supervision)

4) Behavior: Physiological and Emotional (e.g., physical or behavioral problems and effects on academic or vocational performance)

5) Additional Comments (e.g., to substantiate evaluation findings)

6) Recommendations (e.g., within student's school, other educational facilities, outside educational setting) (McCray, 1982, pp. 65-66)

To increase their ease of use by school personnel, assessment report formats could be modeled after similar categories within the career/vocational education plan that is developed on each evaluated student.

Private-for-profit vocational evaluation report formats may not look any different than reports written in other settings. However, the format may be organized to emphasize an employability profile or functional capacities that can be directly matched to previous and potential job profiles and functional requirements. Sink and Field (1981) presented a brief format that stresses the reporting of transferability of skills information. The Vocational Diagnosis and Assessment of Residual Employability (VDARE) technical data report is broken down into three sections:

1. Background (medical, psychological, social, educational, and vocational history; a summary of the unadjusted vocational profile or the pre-injury capabilities);

2. Residual Employability Profile (reporting of present functioning by qualifications profile, and an explanation and interpretation of the profile); and

3. Summary and Impressions (overall impressions of residual employability, and vocational recommendations) (p. 13).

Matheson (1984) recommends a more comprehensive report format to document Work Capacity Evaluation results. As with other formats, modification to meet unique needs is suggested. The basic components of his outline are as follows:

1. Background (name, age, employer, date of injury, etc.; diagnosis; permanent and stationary status; activity/work restrictions; physicians and dates of reports; source and purpose of referral)

2. Evaluation Structure (how evaluee presents himself/herself; current functional status such as assistive devices, medication, handedness, tolerances, symptomatic response to activities, overall health, vocational goals; and structure of the individual evaluation plan as it relates to physical tolerance and tool use)

3. Evaluation Findings (summary of findings with respect to physical tolerance, tool use, and optimal performance; opinion of problem areas, special strengths, and potential to develop specific tolerance)

4. Summary of Recommendations (summarize each of the above three sections). (pp. 129-130)

A General Format

All of the above formats, although not nearly representative of every type of outline, do demonstrate the subtle differences in various reports not only by setting but by length. Each of these formats has a common element; the reports are sectioned off by headings (e.g., Introduction, Results, Recommendations). This partitions the report into logical categories that allow for easier reading and the ability to quickly find pertinent planning information by section. To better understand the vocational evaluation/assessment report format, the following outline is presented:

1. Cover Page - This optional page may contain the facility/unit name and address, the report title (e.g., Report of Vocational Potential, Comprehensive Vocational Evaluation Report), the client's name, referral source, date, a confidentiality statement, and a brief table of contents (particularly if it is a long report). The table of contents could also be included on a separate page immediately following the cover page.

2. Identifying Information - Any amount and type of information may be contained in this section. It is usually placed at the top of the report in list form and broken down by headings (e.g., Client Name, Date of Birth, Social Security Number). A writer may elect not to give certain information, such as the client's address, or may give only partial information, such as town of residence as opposed to full street address. Although evaluators generally use their own discretion regarding what to include in this section, certain referral sources may dictate that specific pieces of information be supplied for identification purposes. For example, vocational assessments conducted on secondary school students may want their grade level, homeroom teacher, and/or program placement under identifying information. Vocational rehabilitation counselors may want the client's case or file number at the top of the report. Insurance carriers may request the date of injury, insurance case number, and employer/company name listed at the beginning. In some instances, a brief listing of past work experiences (e.g., carpenter, cook, truck driver) may be of benefit to the reader).

3. Reason for Referral - This should always be given in the report. Even if the referral question is very general (e.g., what can this person do?), it should either be summarized or stated verbatim. Your report should specifically address and answer these questions in both the body of the report and the summary and recommendations section. For some reports the only format that may be needed is to list each question and answer it, one at a time.

4. Disability Information - The amount of information contained in this section depends on its importance to the evaluator and to the referral source. For example, in situations where disability information can simply be described by a word or phrase (e.g., paraplegia, educably mentally retarded/handicapped), it can be included under Identifying Information, eliminating the need for a Disability Information section. However, when the information and information needs are extensive, then a Disability Information section becomes essential. Data addressing the nature and extent of the disability, restrictions (medical, physical, vocational), medication(s), treatments, and long-term prognosis should be described. In particular, the names of all physicians and allied health providers and dates of their reports that were used in describing disability information must be included. When information is obtained directly from the client or family through an interview or general discussion, it should be worded so that the reader is aware of the source (e.g., Mr. Jones stated that...; the client claims to...). This same process would hold true for client-generated information con-

tained in any other section of the report.

5. <u>Background Information</u> - As with Disability Information, the extensiveness of this section is dependent on its importance to the evaluator and referral source. If the referral agent is in possession of the information and it has limited value to the report and its recommendations, then it can be briefly summarized in a few sentences in this or another section. A more comprehensive treatment of the data may call for subsectioning the information into categories such as psychological, personal, social, family, educational, and/or vocational. Contradictions between information contained in the referral material and that which was collected during evaluation (e.g., interviews, questionnaires) should be presented and discussed in this or other appropriate sections. As a rule, a very detailed review of background information need not be given unless requested.

6. <u>General Impressions</u> - When included in a report, this section allows evaluators to give their initial as well as overall reactions and feelings about a student or client. Although "gut level" reactions have their place, they should be worded cautiously and the reader informed that it was <u>your</u> impression (e.g., it is the impression/feeling/opinion of this evaluator that...). General impressions and descriptions usually include grooming, dress, overall appearance, attendance, affect, and sometimes basic interview results. Quite often, to ensure report brevity, this section is combined with other behavior observation information (refer to #9 Behavior Observations).

7. <u>Tests/Work Samples/Instruments Administered</u> - When this section is used, it simply lists all instruments given to an evaluee, preferably in the order administered. However, this could be combined with the following section as the introductory sentence.

8. <u>Evaluation Results</u> - Presented in this section is a description of the assessment devices along with their purposes and results, and an interpretation of those results. Information concerning psychological and vocational tests, individual work samples and work sample systems, situational assessment, job-site evaluation, interviewing/feedback, behavior observations, readministration, modifications, and overall performance should be included here. Within the report format, this and the recommendations section are the most flexible in terms of organization; and these organization options will be detailed in the following two chapters. Lengthy descriptions may call for a particular arrangement of the data to simplify their reading and use (which will be discussed in detail in Chapters 10 and 11). In shorter reports, the Evaluation Results section may provide no more than a list of instruments administered with corresponding results (e.g., standard scores, scale scores, percentiles, stanines, I.Q. scores, or grade level scores). This listing is concluded with a brief but overall summary of performance and behavior; while a description of the instruments and norm groups used is included as an appendix to the report.

9. <u>Behavior Observations</u> - If any significant behaviors are noted that require more treatment than allowed in the above section, then they should be covered under a separate category. Work, personal, and social habits and characteristics (e.g., interaction, cooperation, following rules and regulations) should be behaviorally described, including specific references to the frequency, duration, and intensity of the activity in question. Such information is particularly important if adjustment or counseling

services are being considered as a possible recommendation. This section should also address any outstanding positive behaviors that would be an asset to rehabilitation, training, and/or placement.

10. Summary - There are many terms that have been used to describe this section. For example, it can serve as an "abstract" or "synopsis" of the evaluation report; it is a "topical review" or "summary statement." Esser (1974, p. 15) states, "In the summary, a composite picture of the client is presented, emphasizing the client's vocational assets as well as limitations." The summary should be no longer than a paragraph, with key sentences from each section organized into a highly informative overview. Rather than rehashing scores and results, the sentences should be more interpretive and conclusive in nature; if need be, the reader can refer to the body of the report for documentation of summary information. In order to keep this section as brief as possible, the writer should primarily focus on identifying vocational assets and vocational limitations. Some reports even subtitle and list assets and vocational limitations separately to allow for a quick review. Although referral questions are often addressed in the Recommendations section, the writer may wish to give them some attention here. Further, if narrative documentation is given for each recommendation as it is written, this could reduce or even eliminate the need for a summary section.

11. Recommendations - Without a doubt, this is the most important section of any vocational evaluation or assessment report; it is what we are all about! Recommendations are so important that two additional chapters are devoted to this subject. Chapter VI has already presented the types of recommendations, and a forthcoming chapter will describe their organization and wording. Whatever recommendations are given, a wide range of alternatives should be provided. Attention must be paid to whether your recommendations deal with the "real" or the "ideal." For example, when jobs are recommended for a client that are not available in the immediate community (the "ideal"), then this should be stated, along with an indication of where they can be found (the "real"). Most importantly, recommendations should answer referral questions if they are to be of any value whatsoever to the referral source.

12. Report Appendices - This final supplemental section of a report can add further information and documentation to a report without increasing the overall length of the narrative itself. In fact, it can serve to reduce content length by referring the reader to an appendix that gives information that would normally have to be described in the body of the report. For example, rather than explaining the purpose and/or process of each test or work sample, along with the different norm groups used, standard description sheets can be attached as an appendix. Instead of listing all test and work sample scores in the body of the report, they can be listed and profiled in the appendix, saving the narrative section for a discussion and interpretation of the results only. Copies of test and behavior observation forms, as well as the report checklist, can be included as an addendum. Whatever is to be used as an appendix or supplement to the report should be left (as with other information) to the discretion of the evaluator and the needs of the referral source.

The above format is designed primarily to give you ideas of the variety of different sections that can be included in a report. In the interest of brevity and good communication, sections of this format can be rearranged, combined, modified, or deleted, and new sections added if necessary.

Conclusion

There are four components of the narrative report: identifying information, body of the report, summary and recommendations, and attachments. Generally speaking, report formats will vary by setting, process, length, outcomes, referral questions, the writer's style, and needs of the referral source. Regardless of the format chosen, all vocational evaluation/assessment reports contain similar kinds of information. The most important part of an evaluation report is the recommendations section, and the key to its overall success is its ability to answer the referral questions.

Chapter X

ORGANIZING THE BODY OF THE REPORT

The Organization Process

As discussed in Chapter VIII, a client's file and the subsequent report writing outline should be arranged in the same order that information will be presented in the report. Of particular concern is the logical organization of the body of the report itself. Proper organization will promote better understanding, interpretation, and utilization of the information provided - the purpose behind all assessment reports. Depending on the amount, type, and purpose of the information to be conveyed, writers may want to organize, or tailor, the body of the data in the shortest narrative possible. Three popular approaches to organizing the body of the report are: the topic outline, performance outcome, and chronological order. All three approaches will be presented throughout the remainder of this chapter.

The Topic Outline

The topic outline approach is frequently used when a large number of instruments are administered, or there is a significant amount of information to be presented. Report content can be sectioned off by the types of instruments and techniques employed. For example, the sub-headings for a report body may read: Interview Results, Psychological Tests, Work Sample Results, Behavior Observations. Another report may use Interest Tests, Dexterity Tests, Aptitude Tests, and Situational Assessment as categories. If a comprehensive psychological or work sample battery is administered, then the name of that test or system can be used as a sub-heading. Avoid beginning with abbreviations or acronyms when identifying a system by name (e.g., General Aptitude Test Battery, instead of GATB).

Another approach to the topic outline is to categorize/divide content by critical outcome areas, rather than by instruments. This technique is incorporated when overlapping results on instruments requires a grouping of data for a more global interpretation of overall outcome. Using sub-headings such as Quality, Quantity, Performance, and Worker Characteristics will allow the evaluator to highlight critical results as they relate to each area (or sub-heading) rather than to each instrument. Functional categories (e.g., motor functioning, cognitive functioning, and critical vocational behaviors/adaptive behaviors) can also be used as sub-headings in a report. Additional functional topics related to communication, sensory functioning, or medical/physical condition can be sub-headed as the need arises. Still another outline might break the content down into three or four simple headings such as: Mental Abilities, Physical Capacities, and Interpretation or Interest, Achievement, Aptitude, and Dexterity. Simpler outlines should be used with smaller amounts of data. Any number of topic headings can be devised to meed specific information needs.

Performance Outcome

The performance outcome approach is commonly used when the evaluator wishes to group and express client functioning by overall results, and not as a category of instruments or characteristics as described in the Topic Outline section. In simpler, less technical terms, the performance outcome approach describes results in reference to "best to worst performance." Sub-headings can be divided into Above Average, Average, and Below Average Performance or Competitive, Borderline, and Noncompetitive Performance. It is generally left to the evaluator's discretion whether to begin with "best" or "worst" performance when organizing the content. The arrangement of information by level of outcome allows the reader to easily and rapidly identify the client's strengths and needs through an orderly review of the sub-headings.

Chronological Order

The chronological approach is used when the order of instrument administration has relevance to the outcome and to the presentation of evaluation data. This sequential approach is similar to the organization and recording of progress notes. Shorter reports, or evaluations, that incorporate a limited number of evaluation instruments might best be served through the chronological approach.

Private-for-profit evaluation reports may also use this organizational approach when documenting the effects that the assessment process has on work tolerance, stamina, and statements of pain and fatigue. The content is arranged in order of first-to-last instrument and technique that was administered. For example, Intake Interview, The ABC Interest Inventory, The Acme Dexterity Test, The Clerical Aptitude Test, Adding Machine Operation Work Sample, and Exit Interview. A description of performance, results, and behavior is given under each sub-heading; and overall evaluation interpretations are presented in the summary and recommendations section at the end (or beginning) of the report.

Combinations of Approaches

There are times when these various approaches to content organization might best serve the needs of the writer when used in combination with each other. In certain instances, an evaluator may wish to organize overall evaluation results using the topic outline approach; then within each sub-heading, arrange specific work sample and tests results using the performance outline or chronological order approach. On the other hand, the evaluator may wish to use the chronological order approach to organize overall assessment content, and the performance outcome approach to present specific test and work sample results.

For example, the first instrument Mary administered to her client was the Differential Aptitude Test (DAT). Since she decided to use the chronological order approach, the DAT was the first sub-heading in the body of the report. Within this sub-heading she grouped and arranged the individual sub-test results by performance outcome (i.e., those DAT sub-tests on which the client scored above average, average, and below average, in that order). In a different report writing situation, Frank decided to use the topic outline approach, thus titling one of his content areas "Dexterity Results." Within this sub-heading, he had two choices for describing individual dexterity test results: the performance outcome or the chronological approach. Under the performance outcome procedure, he could arrange the four dexterity tests that were given from high to low performance. Using the chronological approach, he could list the four dexterity tests in the order given.

Frank decided to incorporate the performance outcome arrangement, under this and other sub-headings, to provide continuity in the overall presentation of results for the reader.

An Example of the Organization Process

The North Carolina Department of Public Instruction, Division of Vocational Education (Special Programs Unit, 1985, pp. 38-39) devised THE CAREER DEVELOPMENT PLAN FOR DISADVANTAGED AND HANDICAPPED STUDENTS, which provides guidance in the implementation of appropriate programs and services. The plan is divided into the seven following parts:

PART I: Identifying Information (Name, Grade, School, Handicapped/Disadvantaged Classification)

PART II: Academic Information (Achievement Test Names and Scores, Reading/Math Grade Levels, Strengths, Weaknesses, Grade Point Average)

PART III: Information on Student's Learning Style (Preferred Learning Style, Mode of Expression, Learning Environment)

PART IV: Vocational Interest (Test, Interview, Observation, Highest Interests, Lowest Interests, Expressed Interests)

PART V: Vocational Aptitudes (Tests, Highest Occupational Potential, Lowest Occupational Potential)

PART VI: Recommendations for Vocational Placement and Supplemental Services (Vocational Program Placement, Supplemental Services Needed, Methods, Person Responsible, Other Resources Needed)

PART VII: Signatures

If an evaluator wanted to provide information in a sequence that could be readily used in developing a plan, similar to the one described above, then the report outline and content should mirror that of the plan. Each section title within the plan could also serve as a sub-heading for the report. This would allow the reader to fill in each part of the plan while that corresponding part of the report is being read. This approach could reduce potential complaints that report contents lack relatedness to the needs of the reader. Further, it will assist in direct and immediate planning with little difficulty in transferring information from the report to the plan, itself. Behavior observations and other pertinent data can be incorporated into existing sections in the report or organized into a separate section if the information requires special treatment.

Conclusion

There are three basic approaches to organizing the body of an evaluation report: the topic outline, performance outcome, and chronological order. The file should be organized in the order in which the report content will be written. This arrangement is dependent upon a number of factors, but should be organized to present the most thorough and logical review of the material in the shortest narrative possible. It might even be necessary to use a combination of approaches to ensure a more efficient arrangement of the content. To aid in the organization of the body of the report, vocational evaluators can rely on documents and forms used by the referral agent in developing client/student plans, and model the report content in the same order and structure as the planning instrument. Such an arrangement will enhance the transfer and use of report information in planning.

Chapter XI

CONTENT OF INSTRUMENT DESCRIPTION

What Goes Where?

When writing up specific test and work sample results in the body of a report, there are almost as many different descriptive formats as there are writers. To save writing time and space in the narrative, many evaluators will often defer descriptions and/or results of instruments to the appendix section to leave the body of the report free for discussion and interpretation of performance. Regardless of its order or location, there is certain information that must be included when describing the instruments used in the assessment process. However, there are exceptions to the rule. Short evaluation reports that may only be geared to listing recommendation options, or situations where a vocational assessment specialist will be using the results to specifically develop a student plan (as opposed to writing a report), may not need to treat the data to the extent described in this chapter. Longer reports may provide detailed descriptions and interpretations of each instrument, or groups of instruments, given during the course of the evaluation. Yet there are other reports that list only the instruments administered, along with their scores, in the body of the report and save the descriptions for the appendix section. In these situations, interpretations are either included at the conclusion of the narrative or in the summary and recommendations section.

What Should be Covered?

There is no need for the write-up of an instrument to be lengthy, unless there is pertinent information to be shared that dictates a need for a detailed explanation. In this case, it is better to sacrifice length for usable information. Several key areas should be covered in describing test and work sample results, either in the body of the report and/or the appendix section: instrument name/title, description of the instrument or task, identification of norm group(s), score(s), behavior observations, other pertinent results (e.g., readministration, accommodation/modification), and overall interpretation. The remainder of this chapter will focus on how to organize and write instrument descriptions and results.

Instrument Name

Every test, task, or work sample that is described in an evaluation report should first be identified by name or title. As mentioned in CHAPTER X, avoid using abbreviations or acronyms when identifying an instrument by name (e.g., Minnesota Rate of Manipulation Tests, instead of MRMT; Crawford Small Parts Dexterity Test, instead of Crawford). In the shortest evaluation reports, the names of instruments are generally given even if descriptions are not.

Descriptions

As a rule, a brief description of the work sample, test, or task is given with its name/title. This description should not exceed one sentence and can often be sufficiently covered in a phrase. For example:

1. The Mail Sorting Work Sample is designed to evaluate an individual's ability to sort 300 envelopes by zip code.

2. To evaluate his reading, spelling, and mathematical ability, Mr. Jones was administered the Wide Range Achievement Test - Revised.

In some instances, the title of the instrument is self-explanatory and may not need a formal description, as is the case with the "Card Filing by Letter and Number Work Sample" and the "Carburetor Disassembly Work Sample." However, if an appendix section is used to accommodate instrument descriptions, then a more lengthy explanation could include not only what it was designed to assess but any related jobs and/or relevant occupational codes (e.g., <u>Dictionary of Occupational Titles</u> codes). Without some indication of what the device is designed to assess, the reader may not know how the results relate to the world of work.

Scores

Scores can be reported in two basic forms: raw scores (e.g., time, errors, correct responses) and converted scores (e.g., percentiles, stanines, scale scores, I.Q., grade level, and predetermined time studies such as Methods Time Measurement). To minimize writing time and verbiage, some evaluators prefer to dispense with raw scores and only concentrate on reporting converted scores. However, there are times when reporting raw scores can best illustrate performance. For example, in an attempt to illustrate a client's physical capacities, Millicent stated, in her evaluation report, that, "Mr. Bond's hand-grip strength, as measured by three trials of the hand dynamometer, averaged 48 pounds placing him in the 15 percentile range when compared to males 25 to 30 years of age." This particular write-up allowed for the presentation of both norm referenced scores (percentiles) and criterion referenced scores (pounds of grip strength) in the same sentence. Frank included in his evaluation report that, "Although this individual was able to complete the work sample with 100% accuracy, it took her 35 minutes longer than the 30-minute time period usually required to complete the test." When timed and untimed scores are reported, the evaluator may want to indicate how many questions were answered in the designated time period and how many additional items were correctly answered when the time limit was extended.

When reporting scores, writers have a number of format options available to them. One option is to include the score within the narrative description. For example: "On the Card Filing by Letter and Number Work Sample, Mortimer filed (5) of the 200 cards incorrectly, resulting in a score around the 80 percentile when compared to clerical job applicants." However, in situations where there are multiple scores to be reported, the evaluator might want to use a more graphic approach and construct a table. For example: when administered all sub-tests of the Purdue pegboard, Darby obtained the following results:

<u>Sub-Test Percentile Scores</u>

NormGroup	Right Hand	Left Hand	Both Hands	Rt.+Left+ Both Hands	<u>Assembly</u>
Industrial Applicants	60-65	55-60	80-85	60-65	99+
Veterans and College Students	45-50	40-45	70	40-45	93-94

Instruments such as the Wide Range Achievement Test - Revised (WRAT-R) could also be listed in table form with sub-headings for standard scores, percentile scores, and grade equivalent scores. In the case of multi-aptitude test batteries, test scores could be grouped and listed by outcome, or type of test, and the results discussed by group. When tables are not used, reporting scores may take no more than a sentence and can be conveniently included with the instrument description. A few evaluators have elected to include scores, along with the instrument descriptions, in the appendix section and only use the body of the report to present outcome and interpretation information. In some instances, they may use descriptive words or statements such as "High, Average, Low" or "Competitive, Borderline, Non-competitive" in lieu of scores to convey performance results, particularly when the scores are contained in the appendix section.

Norm Groups

A common error of evaluators is the failure to describe norm groups used in reporting converted scores. Many tests and commercially available work samples have developed several norm groups to which evaluators can compare their clients, thus expanding the flexibility and utility of the information obtained. To simply report a percentile score without identifying the norm group does not give the reader a frame of reference for evaluating the client's overall performance. If Morgan scored at the 60 percentile on a drafting work sample, the evaluator might assume that it was a potentially competitive score. This might be the case if the norms were based on students in a drafting school. However, if these norms are based on special-needs students in a remedial math class, then the results may give an entirely different picture of Morgan's potential to succeed in a formal drafting curriculum. Therefore, in some instances, scores may be reported and compared against several different norm groups in order to give the reader a clearer picture of how the client performed in relation to various settings. Norm group information can easily be given in the same sentence (or on the same table) with score data and other instrument descriptions, as illustrated in the above examples. As with instrument descriptions and scores, some evaluators have chosen to include norm group information in the appendix section.

Behavior Observations

Descriptions of positive or negative client behaviors must be included if they potentially influenced performance or could have an impact on training or employment. This information is particularly important to counselors and work adjustment personnel when a recommendation for services such as work adjustment, counseling, or selective/prescriptive placement is being considered. Your report should serve as a vehicle for establishing a behavioral baseline to guide work adjustment planning and goal development. Special attention should be given to documenting the frequency, duration, and intensity/severity/magnitude of the behavior in question (Botterbusch, 1984). Pertinent client statements regarding their feelings, attitudes, impressions, and opinions should be included. Statements such as "I hate this test," "I don't like to read," "This was the most interesting thing I have taken so far," could be quoted in the write-up. Behaviors that vary from one instrument to another, or from the beginning to the end of evaluation, may deserve individual treatment in their own section, rather than with each instrument.

In addition to the considerations described above, Dunn (1973) provides additional guidelines for documenting observations:

1. Describe behaviors in observable terms.

2. Describe the situation in which the behavior occurred.

3. Use action verbs whenever possible.

4. Use a terse, direct style.

For the most part, descriptions and brief interpretations of behavioral observations associated with a particular instrument may take no more than one or two sentences, depending on their complexity.

The following examples are provided to illustrate just a few of the many ways that specific behavior observations can be written.

Every time someone entered the room (approximately four times during this 30-minute test), Karl would look up and stop what he was doing until the evaluator reminded him to return to work. This poor distraction tolerance was exhibited on all other tasks he was administered.

Ms. White's low score on the Card Filing Work Sample could be due, in part, to her frequent dozing throughout the task. When asked why she could not stay awake, she stated that she liked to watch late night television movies.

Ramone's frequent statements of interest in this line of work were consistent with his high level of attention span during the course of this and other related work samples.

It is important to remember that all interpretations of behaviors should be documented with a description of the behavior and the situation in which it occurred.

Readministration and Modification

In a few instances, special assessment accommodations will need to be made for an individual. A work sample may be readministered to determine if the evaluee can improve performance or reach criterion over repeated trials. The administrative approach and/or physical arrangement of an instrument may be modified to accommodate a particular disability. In any case, these changes must be shared with the readers to let them know the conditions under which the client performed. These changes can be translated into prescriptions for modification or accommodation in training, working, or living conditions to enhance overall performance. If an individual is unable to take an instrument as it is intended, other similar instruments will need to be administered or the existing one modified to meet the client's unique needs. Although results will more than likely be contaminated, modifications in assessment devices will allow evaluators to make recommendations for comparable accommodations in training and jobs. This provides input on the specific kinds of changes that should be considered beyond the evaluation process.

In reporting such changes, the evaluator should state why the modification is needed, what was modified and how, and what resulted in terms of outcome. Readministration of an instrument should state why, and how many times, readministration is being conducted; how the final results compare to the initial results; and what this means to possible placement considerations. These special conditions will only be necessary in a few cases, but the evaluator must always be prepared to provide and report such accommodations.

To illustrate the descriptive process of readministration and modification, the following examples are provided as only one of several ways to deal with the results.

Although Ms. Wong expressed an interest in a mail-sorting position, she scored around the 25 percentile on time, with no errors, on the Mail Sorting by Zip Code Work Sample when compared to employed worker norms. When given an opportunity to retake the work sample, with the goal of improving her speed, she increased her time score to around the 55 percentile, but also committed three errors, placing her around the 75 percentile on accuracy. If given sufficient time to learn and practice a mail-sorting job, Ms. Wong has the potential to function competitively.

Paul stated that he was unable to follow the written directions that accompanied the Cash Register Work Sample. Therefore, the material was read to him and his comprehension verified on the practice trial. The resulting performance placed him within the 95 percentile range on both speed and accuracy, indicating potential to operate a cash register in environments where job-related reading is not required.

Due to her upper extremity impairment, Mrs. Gonzales was unable to appropriately mark the IBM answer sheet on the interest inventory. To overcome this problem, she was allowed to dictate the item number and answer into a voice-activated tape recorder; and the responses later converted to an answer sheet for scoring purposes.

The complex nature of these procedures may require several sentences to fully explain the purposes and outcomes of the modification or readministration in question. Implications for training and employment could be addressed either in the body of the report or the recommendations section. Since these techniques are not frequently performed, the evaluator may find that extensive write-ups will be an exception to the rule.

Overall Interpretation

Many evaluators often wait until the end of a section, or the end of the report, itself, before interpreting overall performance. Often, the only interpretation that an evaluator might be able to make is the level of performance achieved and what instrument(s) should be administered next based on previous outcome. In those situations where a particular work sample warrants a special interpretation, one or two sentences may provide sufficient coverage. Interpretations, themselves, generally relate to two areas: client performance and behavior. In some instances, comparing results and/or client statements from one test or work sample to several other instruments, or to information from the file or intake interview, will provide a stronger case for an evaluator's interpretation. As previously mentioned, interpretations should never be given without some form of documentation (e.g., score's, client statements, behavior observations).

To exemplify this interpretive process, the following illustrations are presented.

Mr. Rogers' stated interest for employment in the performing arts is consistent with his previous work history and interest test results.

Darby's above-average dexterity test results on the Purdue Pegboard are inconsistent with her below-average performance on the Minnesota Rate of Manipulation Tests (MRMT). Reasons that could account for this discrepancy relate to the fact that: the tests measure two different types of dexterity, fine finger and manual dexterity, respectively. She had taken medicine for a cold prior the administration of the MRMT, and Darby had some difficulty learning how to take the MRMT.

Due to Bob's poor accuracy and handwriting on the Measuring Skills Test, it was decided not to administer him the Drafting Work Sample. It is the opinion of this evaluator that his expressed interest for a career in mechanical drafting might be unrealistic until he is able to remediate the above deficiencies.

Examples of interpretations of readministration and modification were described in the previous section. Please remember that in many instances, very little, if any, interpretation will be needed for most individual instruments administered; and this activity is usually reserved for the end of the report as an "overall interpretation" of evaluation results.

Reporting Results: An Example

An efficient instrument write-up should generally take one or two sentences to give the name/title, description, scores, and norm groups for each work sample or test. One or two sentences for behavioral, modification, and/or readministration information and an additional sentence or two for an overall interpretation, when needed, should provide adequate coverage of the subject matter. One final example will be given using two different approaches. The first illustration is highly narrative and provides the reader with a detailed description of client performance.

> Based on her expressed interest in bookkeeping, Ms. Chase was administered the Payroll Computation Work Sample to evaluate her ability to compute hourly wages from a time card with an adding machine and enter the amount on a ledger. When compared to the unselected employed worker norm group, Mary scored above the 90 percentile (only one error) on accuracy and between the 35-40 percentile on speed. She has been consistently slow but accurate on all clerical tasks, indicating potential for vocational training as a bookkeeper or entry level placement in a clerical position, where she will be given ample time to learn the task and reach a competitive performance rate.

The above description only took three sentences to complete and could be shortened by transferring the interpretive information to the end of the report or the summary and recommendations sections. The same case will now be presented using a more abbreviated approach. Although this technique is less narrative, many evaluators consider it to be quicker and easier to read and write.

Title: Payroll Computation Work Sample (refer to appendix for description).

Norm Group: Unselected employed workers.

Percentile: Accuracy 90+
              Speed   35-40

Comments: Expressed an interest in bookkeeping. Slow but accurate on all clerical tasks.

Recommendation: Vocational training as a bookkeeper or entry level placement in a clerical position, where she will be given ample time to learn the task and reach a competitive performance rate.

Conclusion

When profiling the instruments administered, the vocational evaluation report should attempt to give their name/title, assessment description, identification of norm group(s), score(s), behavior observations, other pertinent results (e.g., readministration, accommodation/modification), and overall interpretation. Although the length of each test and work sample narrative generally runs from three to five sentences, it can be reduced by placing the instrument descriptions (and, in some cases, norm groups and tests cores) in the appendix section. Further, interpretations of performance can be provided after each instrument, at the end of the section, within its own section, or in the summary and recommendations section. Likewise, behavior observations can be described in a number of places depending on their extensiveness. It is the body of the report and the evaluation of results section that are used to document report recommendations.

Chapter XII

WRITING PRESCRIPTIVE RECOMMENDATIONS

What is a Prescriptive Recommendation?

Without hesitation, recommendations are the most important part of any vocational evaluation/assessment report. Regardless of how well the body of the report is organized and written, if the recommendations do not provide practical guidance in planning, then the report serves as no more than an academic exercise. Many of the problems with reports, as discussed in CHAPTER IV, relate to poorly developed recommendations. In particular, counselors were concerned that recommendations did not provide enough specificity, or prescriptive detail, to direct effective rehabilitation/education services. Therefore, the process of formulating prescriptive recommendations should become an integral part of any report-writing activity.

The vocational evaluation process must be set up to yield prescriptive information that can later be translated into prescriptive recommendations (Bates, 1981; Leland and Rice, 1982; Rice, 1972). To illustrate this point, Rice (1972) states that:

> The primary concern of vocational evaluation should be to ensure all clients the most valid and reliable evaluation program possible. In order to achieve this goal and to prescribe the most appropriate services, vocational evaluators must first identify the rehabilitation problems and gain an in-depth understanding of the rehabilitation needs of each individual client. The evaluator must diagnose such major problem areas as to why the client cannot function independently or why he is not ready to engage in remunerative employment. He must then determine the specific types of services that are essential to alleviate or reduce the handicapping effects of these problems. (p. 8)

Leland and Rice (1982) present further detail concerning what prescriptive information should be included in the evaluation/assessment report.

> The established objectives for the prescription should be supported by facts, observations, test results, client and counselor concurrence, and other pertinent data. Short-term objectives should be developed and continuously evaluated for redirection toward the acquisition of established long-range goals. In addition, the prescriptive evaluation identifies who, how, and in what sequence the services are to be delivered (p. 74)...Using the prescriptive approach, the vocational evaluator provides the referring counselor with a report that includes vocational, personal, social, and other traditional information and a "prescription" for services that will meet the client's individual needs with reference to identified assets and deficits. The report includes a sequential plan of action, as appropriate, for improving behavior, developing work potential, reducing educational deficits, and improving personal relations, personal appearance, and so on...the prescriptive evaluation report develops both short- and long-range goals in order of priority; the programs needed; the specific services to be emphasized; and, if possible, the approach that the staff should use in working with the client. (p. 80)

Not all report recommendations will be able to cover prescriptions in such depth. However, evaluators should continuously strive to provide as much detail and direction as possible. To begin the process of formulating report recommendations, the evaluator will want to refer back to CHAPTER VI for critical guidance in two areas: (1) developing recommendation options and (2) completing the recommendation checklist. By engaging in these activities, the evaluator will ensure that the best possible recommendations will be developed. The remainder of this chapter will focus on the specific considerations and steps that should be followed in writing meaningful prescriptive recommendations.

List Recommendations in Priority Order

An important rule in writing prescriptive recommendations is to begin with short-term recommendations and conclude with long-term ones (Rice, 1972). The successful attainment of long-range goals is often dependent upon the positive completion of specific short-range objectives. This method of prioritizing recommendations allows the writer to list the most immediate and important need first. For example, a recommendation for further assessment of physical capacities might precede a recommendation for client placement in a dock-loading position; a recommendation for remediation in change making would pre-empt training in retail sales or cash-register operation; grooming skills should be improved before job placement as a bank teller is considered. In some instances, the sequential ordering of recommendations (i.e., making the attainment of one recommendation contingent upon the other) may be the only way in which services can be successfully rendered.

Prioritize Probable Jobs, Training, and Services

When there are a number of jobs, training options, and services available to a client, evaluators might have difficulty deciding which ones to list first. There are a number of methods that can be used in prioritizing recommendation options, and the following are four such methods that are available to the assessment specialist.

1. <u>List jobs/training/services by level of interest</u>. Starting with high interest recommendations and proceeding to those of lesser interest to the client, the evaluator is providing the reader with a placement hierarchy that is indexed by potential levels of success.

2. <u>List jobs/training/services by level of availability</u>. There is greater assurance of success if those areas that are more readily available can be listed first and given priority for placement. Also critical to the issue of availability is the proximity of the site to the student/client. Local jobs, training, and services should be given priority over those located so far away as to require relocation. The controversy over whether to list jobs outside the client's immediate community has long been an issue with assessment specialists, since these types of recommendations border somewhere between the "real" and the "ideal." To make recommendations for jobs, training, or services outside the client's community more palatable, they should be accompanied by a statement indicating where they can be found. Further, the issue of relocation will also need to be resolved before the recommendation can be considered as having any value or merit.

3. <u>Prioritize job recommendations by salary/wage scale</u>. In situations where an individual needs to earn a certain income in order to exceed disability or welfare payments, or to support dependents, then the highest paying jobs should be listed first.

4. <u>Enumerate recommendations by cost-effectiveness</u>. In some instances, a lack of time and/or funds may prohibit the initiation of complex plans that require extensive services. Therefore, the evaluator may want

to provide the referral source with a variety of recommendation options that range in cost and comprehensiveness. For example, a client who demonstrates outstanding accounting skills might be recommended for a more expensive and time-consuming plan that would optimize her abilities, such as enrollment in a Bachelor's Degree program in accounting. A less costly and extensive plan for enrollment in a business school or community college accounting program could also be recommended as an alternative. One additional recommendation, which is the cheapest and most efficient to implement, would call for on-the-job training in an entry-level accounting clerk position. Unless specified in a referral question, the ordering of these kinds of recommendations should be left to the evaluator's discretion. Listing all possible recommendations, regardless of time or cost requirements, provides the user with an active range of placement options. If one recommendation is not appropriate or feasible, or does not prove successful, then other options are available to the reader.

The writer may find that combinations of these methods will improve the probability of placement success. For example, recommendations may be prioritized by interest and job/training/service availability; salary and cost-effectiveness; interest and salary; or job/training/service availability and cost-effectiveness. In considering which methods to combine, the evaluator should choose the ones that prioritize and order recommendations from their highest to lowest "probabilities for success." Regardless of the combinations used, evaluators have an obligation to ensure that all placement possibilities for their students and clients are translated into feasible recommendations. If there are a number of options available to a client, it is not necessarily the evaluator's responsibility to decide which one(s) should be included and which one(s) should be left out but to see to it that a realistic range of potential recommendations and plans is systematically listed in the report. Although informed evaluator opinion is an integral part of any recommendation, the final decision concerning direction rests with the referral source and client.

Separate Recommendations

To improve readability, all recommendations should be listed in numerical order and/or separated by spaces (i.e., separate sentences or paragraphs). When one continuous narrative is used to list and describe individual recommendations, the information may tend to run together, making it difficult for the reader to sort out pertinent facts and plans of action. It is also quite easy to lose one's place, as a result of having to continuously refer back to a run-on recommendation section, while attempting to use the assessment report as a resource document during plan development. When recommendations can be both separated and prioritized, as described above, it lends order to the section and increases its utility and efficiency.

Use a General-to-Specifics Approach

Evaluators have long experienced difficulty trying to meet the varied needs of a wide range of referral sources. In particular, not all counselors or teachers want recommendations written the same way. To illustrate this point, let us examine the problem as it applies to job-related recommendations.

Some referral agents may only want the evaluator to list potential job areas, clusters, or families that might be available to the client. On the other hand, another referral source may request specific job titles, and accompanying <u>Dictionary of Occupational Titles</u> codes, to be listed instead of global or generic placement recommendations. To overcome this problem and meet the needs of all users within the same recommendation, the assessment specialist may want to incorporate the "general-to-specific approach" when writing recommendations. This can be accomplished by simply listing both the job family and the specific job title(s), and codes if necessary, when a recommendation for employment is tendered. For example:

> Gwen should be considered for entry level placement in a general clerical position such as file clerk, mail clerk, routing clerk, or related job.

This technique works equally well with education, training, and adjustment services. For example:

> Ms. Edwards demonstrates both high interest and competitive potential for community college training in a medical service field that would allow for patient contact. An Associate Degree in areas such as nursing, occupational or physical therapy assistant, radiologic technology, or respiratory therapy is recommended. All programs are available at the local community college, with the exception of respiratory therapy, which is offered through Glover County College, approximately 100 miles north of her home.

List Alternatives

As previously mentioned, the evaluator should attempt to list as many alternative recommendations as possible. If one is not feasible, then there are other options to choose from, given that the writer has taken the time to include them in the report. If only one recommendation is listed, and cannot be implemented, then the report may no longer serve anyone's needs. As long as there are plans of action to work with, then the report will continue to serve the purpose for which it was intended. Alternatives should be developed in three major areas.

1. Jobs - List more than one job when possible. In addition, list the type of placement being recommended (e.g., direct, selective, prescriptive, supported work, full-time, part-time). In some situations, the type of placement assistance (e.g., job coaching, job club) may need to be specified.

2. Training/Education - List all potential training and education options, such as vocational/industrial/business trades curriculums, on-the-job training, apprenticeship programs, trade or business schools, adult education, community/junior colleges, and university undergraduate or graduate curriculums that are available to the student or client. Of equal importance to the level of training is identification of the area of study (or major) that should be considered.

3. Services - There are any number of available personal, social, remedial, and vocational adjustment services that can be recommended for a client. Along with recommending individual services, the evaluator should also consider listing "combinations" of services when necessary. Activities that can be offered concurrently not only save time and money but increase the likelihood that the established plan will reach successful fruition. For example, an evaluator may recommend a client for family counseling to deal with frequent family fighting, while at the same time making a referral to work adjustment to improve his/her production skills. Another client might receive simultaneous recommendations for entry level daytime employment in a cafeteria, placement in a community living situation or half-way house until independent living skills can be improved, and GED preparation classes at night to improve long-range job potential.

Specify Contingencies

The vocational evaluator should specify all conditions, stipulations, and circumstances surrounding successful placement. If these prescriptions are not followed, then the chances for success are greatly diminished. Contingencies should be used to guide the placement process as it relates to appropriate modification and accommodation. For example, part of a prescriptive recommendation might read as follows:

> Placement as a cashier in a small, low-volume business should be considered. Due to Sheldon's below-average speed on the Cash Register Work Sample, it would be best to avoid highly production-oriented environments, such as large grocery and discount stores, until sufficient on-the-job experience has been gained to improve his speed.

Use Narrative Descriptions

When necessary, a detailed narrative description of the recommendation should replace short statements or phrases. Highly descriptive recommendations could shorten or even replace the report summary. It is essential that narrative descriptions be used when a concise statement fails to explain the prescriptive needs of the client. For example:

> Although Ms. Navabi has the reading comprehension necessary to succeed in the aforementioned business curriculum, her below-average reading speed may create problems in adequately completing overnight assignments and timed tests. Therefore, it is recommended that she receive a remedial reading course designed to improve her speed, prior to enrollment in business school.

Justify Recommendations

As covered in CHAPTER IX, the body of the report is primarily used to document and justify the recommendations. However, there may be complex or questionable recommendations that, by their unique nature, require extensive explanation and narrative support in order to "convince" referral sources of their viability. For example:

> In spite of Mr. O'Brien's visual impairment, he demonstrated exceptionally high intelligence and achievement levels. Further, his equally high levels of interest and aptitude for computer programming make him an excellent candidate for training in this area. This would require an appropriately modified training and working environment, including Braille reference materials and voice-synthesized computer equipment. Referral to a rehabilitation engineer to develop the necessary modifications is strongly recommended.

Even in situations where recommendations are not complex or questionable, additional narrative detail will make understanding and implementing the recommendation much easier. As mentioned above, it may also shorten the report body and/or summary section. A recommendation for a particular rehabilitation service should always specify (i.e., document, justify) what problem needs attention. For example:

> Work adjustment services that can reduce Morgan's frequent tardiness are recommended.

Specific scores or frequency counts of behavior need not be included in a recommendation as long as they are contained in the body of the report or appendix. However, very detailed, supportive data should always accompany the report to give service providers an idea of the magnitude of the problem and a base line from which to start. If the evaluator used a technique during the assessment process that had a positive effect on the behavior, this, too, is worthy of mentioning, along with any positive behaviors that can be an asset to the provision of rehabilitation/education services.

Avoid Using Absolutes

As stated in CHAPTER III, "Do not

use absolutes unless absolutely sure." This is just as true with recommendations as it is with the body of the report. Describing any form of placement in terms of "probabilities of success" will help you avoid making false positive or false negative statements. To matter-of-factly state that your client absolutely can or cannot do something requires you to accept responsibility for all unforeseen circumstances and variables (e.g., high or low motivation, job layoffs, fluctuating unemployment rates that make jobs easier or more difficult to obtain, and personality conflicts between the client and supervisor or co-workers).

Without sounding completely noncommittal, evaluators can provide the reader with excellent placement information while avoiding the use of dichotomies such as "can" or "cannot," "absolutely" or "never." To do so, we must couch recommendations in terms that imply "a reasonable degree of vocational probability." For example, it would be more appropriate to say that "Barny has a high probability of being employed as a police officer," instead of "Barny can be employed as a police officer." Rather than stating, "Ms. Tomlin cannot be a telephone operator," it would be preferable to say, "Due to her serious speech impediment, Ms. Tomlin's chances for successful employment are quite limited at the present time," or "Until Ms. Tomlin's serious speech impediment can be rectified, her chances for successful employment as a telephone operator will remain low."

There are times when contrasting the potential of two jobs would clarify placement priority. This is particularly true when a referral question asks if an individual could be successfully trained for or placed in a specific job. For example:

At present, Nadia's chances for successful vocational training are higher in computer operation than they are in computer programming.

Although additional wording can further explain this recommendation, it does provide the reader with a specific placement priority.

Conclusion

The most critical part of any vocational evaluation/assessment report is the recommendation section. Recommendations should be prescriptive in nature. That is, they should identify the problem, rehabilitation/education/job placement needs, and a plan of services that will lead to success. The systematic ordering of prescriptive recommendations will allow the service provider to choose plans that will realistically meet the client's needs, as they relate to levels of interest, job/training/service availability, income level, probabilities for success, and cost-effectiveness. By listing the most immediate needs first and progressing to more long-range goals, prioritized recommendations provide important guidance in the delivery of effective rehabilitation and education services.

Chapter XIII

EVALUATING YOUR REPORT

When to Evaluate Your Report

Once you have finished writing your vocational assessment report, please keep in mind that the communication process is not yet complete. To ascertain the effectiveness of your report in relaying meaningful, vocationally related information, it should be evaluated through several different approaches. Evaluations of reports are conducted at various times, depending on the type of information you are trying to collect. For example, if an assessment specialist wants to determine if a report is grammatically and syntactically sound, technically accurate, well organized, and logical, then reports should be evaluated before they are made available to the referral source. If a vocational evaluator would like to know how effective the report was in meeting the needs of the client/student and referral agent, then a follow-up and critique should be conducted after it has been used as a planning document. This final chapter will address the various issues of report evaluation and suggest strategies and approaches for systematically determining the effectiveness of written communication. In particular, five evaluation considerations will be examined:

1. writing style;
2. accuracy;
3. technical quality;
4. utility; and,
5. outcome.

What Needs to be Evaluated?

Both internal and external forms of report evaluations are available to the assessment specialist. Internal evaluations refer to an in-house examination of writing style, accuracy, and technical quality of the report before it is finalized. External evaluations survey the usefulness of the report to the counselor or teacher and its relationship to case outcome. External evaluations are generally conducted as a routine part of client/student follow-up and program evaluation. The following is a detailed explanation of the five report evaluation considerations.

1. WRITING STYLE - Chapter I addressed the subject of using good grammar and syntax in report writing. After an assessment report has been written, it should be proofed for correct wording, punctuation, use of tense, spelling, sentence and paragraph structure, continuity, and all other writing qualities that represent a good command of the English language. Some evaluators are fortunate to have secretaries who are "sticklers" for editorial detail. Others who use word processors may rely on software packages that can check spelling and hyphenation. In any event, writing style should be evaluated regularly to ensure report quality and provide the writer with guidelines for improving communication skills.

2. ACCURACY - Immediately after final typing, a report should be carefully checked for accuracy. Names, addresses, dates, ages, file/case numbers, codes, disabilities, and scores should be examined for correctness. Mistyping a "3" instead of an "8" or a "9" for a "7" could create substantial problems when reporting grade level, IQ, or percentile scores.

3. TECHNICAL QUALITY - This more abstract consideration refers to the report's ability: be objective; present sound, well-documented, and justified conclusions from available information; draw an accurate "picture" of what the client is like and his/her

vocational assets and limitations; and be believable and realistic. In addition, the report should be well organized and logical in the presentation of data that leads to the formulation of conclusive outcomes and directions. CHAPTER IV suggests a technique whereby a supervisor or fellow evaluator would read selected reports to critique, among other things, their technical quality. This kind of third-party review can provide a writer with highly constructive guidance for the improvement of future reports.

4. UTILITY - Once the referring agent (e.g., counselor, teacher) has had time to read and act on the information in the report, the vocational evaluator is now ready to conduct a follow-up. A major part of this follow-up should focus on the extent to which the report was used in plan development. It is hoped that the user found the report realistic and practical enough to warrant extensive application of the recommendations, as well as the body of the report, in plan development. Before we can determine how accurate the report was in influencing success, we must first establish the fact that it was employed in plan development. Without this assurance, then any further evaluation of report effectiveness is pointless. Referral sources must have enough faith in the assessment reports they receive to use them in the planning process. To say that reports provide viable information just because evaluation units continue to receive clients fails to take into account that referrals are not always made on the basis of the quality of services (i.e., there is no other evaluation service available; referral agents are only allowed to use a particular evaluation unit; the evaluation is a free service to the referral agent; the assessment unit serves as a holding pattern for the student/client until other services can be planned or become available).

5. OUTCOME - Once it has been determined that the report was used in planning, the concluding step in the report evaluation process is relating student/client success to the recommendations. The final chapter in any rehabilitation/education process is successful placement; and if the assessment report has done its job, then its contributions to this positive outcome can be documented. The evaluator should be able to prove that client outcome is related to one or more of the recommendations in the report. The degree of relationship between report content and final case outcome that is needed to validate the true effectiveness of recommendations has never been clearly established.

For example, if an evaluation report recommends that an individual be employed in an entry-level service position but instead that person was successfully placed in an entry-level factory job, could it be said that the report contributed to case outcome? More specifically, does a recommendation for employment or training need to directly relate to the resulting placement before it is considered as having an impact on success? Some evaluators and referring agents feel that as long as a report indicates a person is job or training ready, the specific type of placement is not as important as the fact that the general placement theme was followed. The concern with conducting follow-up based on the absolute recommendation is that evaluators will again be required to accept responsibility for situational and environmental factors beyond their control. In cases where enrollment in a university program is concerned, follow-up will take at least four years before report success can be established. Regardless of the follow-up philosophy observed, the success of the report in guiding and predicting outcome is fundamental to the vocational assessment process.

Developing Report Evaluation Strategies

INTERNAL EVALUATIONS - To aid in the internal evaluation of reports, writers may want to consider the development and use of simple checklists for systematic guidance in this process. Again, the assessment specialist can go back to the original report-writing outline and use it as a guide for report evaluation. Although elements of writing style and accuracy cannot easily be incorporated into such an outline, issues of technical quality can. Questions that should be considered for inclusion in an internal report evaluation form are:

- Does the report provide a clear and accurate picture of the client?

- Were all referral questions answered satisfactorily?

- Are vocational assets and limitations specified, along with realistic and alternative plans of action?

- Are recommendations well documented and feasible?

Any number of rating scales can be added to the outline to help determine the level of compliance with each item. For example, descriptive categories such as Satisfactory and Unsatisfactory, Acceptable and Unacceptable, or Adequate and Insufficient will allow the rater to decide what may need rewriting. If the report writing outline is used for rating purposes, then the Recommendation Checklist described in CHAPTER VI should also be incorporated into the rating process.

Due to limited evaluator time, it may be impractical to develop and use an outline for an internal rating of every report that is written. Therefore, reports could be randomly chosen for rating; or, immediately after writing each one, the evaluator could re-read it while referring back to the report outline and make mental notes (or written comments in the margin of the outline) concerning what needs to be changed.

EXTERNAL EVALUATIONS - Although the use of checklists with internal report evaluations is optional, external evaluations should always rely on a rating form for documentation purposes. As previously mentioned, external evaluations are generally conducted as a part of the follow-up and program evaluation process. Developing a personalized rating form will enable the procedure to be customized to meet the highly specific needs of each writer, referring agent, and the program evaluation process. External rating forms should be concise. That is, they should contain a limited number of questions that can be answered by simply checking the most appropriate response. The rater would be given the option of writing succinct comments when necessary. If the forms are exceedingly long or complicated, the rater may not be willing to take the time to complete and return them. As discussed earlier, two distinctly separate issues need to be examined: has the report been used in planning? If so, was the disposition of the case similar to what was recommended? Since it is generally accepted that an evaluation of a report's usefulness in planning be conducted before the final evaluation of outcome, two separate forms may be needed.

The first form, designed to evaluate technical quality and report utility, could be attached to the outgoing report to be completed immediately following the planning phase. This form should be designed to evaluate the referral source's satisfaction with the report and the extent to which it was used in planning. Questions that could focus on the relationship of the document to planning are:

- Is the report well written and understandable (i.e., gives a clear and accurate picture of the client and indicates what should be done)?

- Does the report answer referral questions?

- Are recommendations realistic, feasible, practical, and appropriately documented?

- What recommendations have been and/or will be used in planning?

Some rating forms list the specific recommendations made for the client and ask the counselor to check those items that were used in planning. Other forms only contain general statements (e.g., placement, training, work adjustment) for the rater to check, which are matched up with the actual report recommendations after they have been returned. Descriptive statements or scales, presented earlier, that are used to rate each question should also be incorporated into the external evaluation form for rating ease and convenience. This should also be accompanied by space for any necessary comments. As previously mentioned, if the rating form is too long or difficult to complete, then chances are it will not be returned.

It is difficult to know exactly when a referral source should be contacted concerning the final follow-up of student/client outcome (e.g., 30, 60, or 90 days; six to twelve months). This is dependent on how quickly job placement can be effected and how long the person needs to remain employed before it is classified as a placement success (e.g., vocational rehabilitation clients must be employed for 60 days before the case can be closed as a successful rehabilitation). Ideally, follow-up rating forms should be completed with all other final paperwork by the referral sources at the time of case closure. Follow-up may simply ask if job placement was successful, or it may try to determine how closely the specific recommendation matched the obtained job. Whatever approach is used depends, to a great extent, on the time and energy of the vocational evaluator and referral source.

Mailing evaluation forms to the referral source is not always the best means of obtaining feedback on a report. Making a telephone or personal contact with the referring teacher or counselor or discussing planning or outcome results during a staffing is an excellent way to collect pertinent data. To maximize information gathering, some assessment specialists contact referral sources by telephone if the report evaluation form that was previously mailed out is not returned. This way, not every individual is called, only those who do not return the rating form. Assessment specialists who are located in the same settings where a client/student will receive additional services (e.g., sheltered workshops, schools, rehabilitation facilities, institutions) will find it considerably easier to conduct external evaluations, due to the ready access of in-house, follow-up data.

Results of all internal and external evaluations should direct the writer in the systematic improvement of reports. Without this solicited feedback from users, assessment specialists will continue to function in a vacuum and eventually come to doubt the value of their work.

Conclusion

The last phase of the report-writing process is an evaluation of the report itself. Areas to be evaluated are writing style, accuracy, technical quality, utility, and outcome. Internal forms of report evaluation are conducted in-house before it is made available to the referral source. The internal evaluation focuses on issues of writing style, accuracy, and technical quality. External forms of report evaluation are conducted by the referral sources once they have received and used the report. The external evaluation focuses on issues of technical quality, utility (i.e., was the report used in planning?), and outcome (i.e., did the report contribute to successful placement?). The goal of this evaluation process is to determine the effectiveness of reports in meeting the needs of student/clients and their referral agents and to systematically guide the assessment specialist in improving overall writing skills.

BIBLIOGRAPHY

Ballantyne, D. (1985). *Cooperative programs for transition from school to work*. Washington, DC: U.S. Department of Education, National Institute of Handicapped Research.

Bates, L. (1981). *Vocational evaluation of severely physically impaired individuals: Considerations and techniques*. Menomonie, WI: University of Wisconsin-Stout, Stout Vocational Rehabilitation Institute, Research and Training Center.

Blakemore, T. F., McCray, P. M., & Coker, C. C. (1985). *A national survey of computer use in rehabilitation facilities*. Menomonie, WI: University of Wisconsin-Stout, Stout Vocational Rehabilitation Institute, Research and Training Center.

Botterbusch, K. F. (1982). *A comparison of commercial vocational evaluation systems (second edition)*. Menomonie, WI: University of Wisconsin-Stout, Stout Vocational Rehabilitation Institute, Materials Development Center.

Botterbusch, K. F. (1984). *Revised MDC behavior identification form*. Menomonie, WI: University of Wisconsin-Stout, Stout Vocational Rehabilitation Institute, Materials Development Center.

Botterbusch, K. F. (1983). *Short-term vocational evaluation*. Menomonie, WI: University of Wisconsin-Stout, Stout Vocational Rehabilitation Institute, Materials Development Center.

Coffey, D. D., Hansen, G. M., Menz, F. E., & Coker, C. C. (1978). *Vocational evaluator role and function as perceived by practitioners and educators*. Menomonie, WI: University of Wisconsin-Stout, Stout Vocational Rehabilitation Institute, Research and Training Center.

Coffey, D. D. (1977). Report writing in vocational (work) evaluation. In W. A. Pruitt, *Vocational (work) evaluation*. Menomonie, WI: Walt Pruitt Associates, 213-221.

Cohen, C., & Bergman, M. (1984). School and community rehabilitation facility cooperation for vocational evaluation services. *Vocational Evaluation and Work Adjustment Bulletin*, 17(4), 140-143.

Commission on Accreditation of Rehabilitation Facilities. (1984). *Standards manual for facilities serving people with disabilities*. Tucson, AZ: Author.

Commission on Certification of Work Adjustment and Vocational Evaluation Specialists. (1986). *Standards and procedures manual for certification maintenance*. Arlington Heights, IL: Author.

Deutch, P. M., & Sawyer, H. W. (1985). *Guide to rehabilitation*. New York, NY: Matthew Bender.

Dunn, D. J. (1973). Recording observations. *Consumer brief*, 1(1).

DuRand, J., & Neufeld, A. (1980). Comprehensive vocational services. In R. Flynn, & K. Wilson, (Eds.), <u>Normalization, social integration, and community service</u>. Baltimore, MD: University Park Press.

Ellis, C. (1985). The vocational evaluator as expert witness. In C. Smith, & R. Fry, (Eds.), <u>National forum on issues in vocational assessment (the issues papers)</u> pp. 62-68). Menomonie, WI: University of Wisconsin-Stout, Stout Vocational Rehabilitation Institute, Materials Development Center.

Ellsworth, S. M., & Noll, A. J. (1978). <u>Vocational evaluators in school settings: Task analysis, certification, qualification and status data</u>. Menomonie, WI: University of Wisconsin-Stout, Stout Vocational Rehabilitation Institute.

Esser, T. J. (1974). <u>Effective report writing in vocational evaluation and work adjustment programs</u>. Menomonie, WI: University of Wisconsin-Stout, Department of Rehabilitation and Manpower Services, Materials Development Center.

Field, T. F., & Sink J. M. (1981). <u>The vocational expert</u>. Athens, GA: VSB, Inc.

Gunning, R. (1953). <u>The technique of clear writing</u>. New York, NY: McGraw-Hill.

Gust, T. (1967). The psychological-vocational evaluation report: Reciprocal referral responsibility. <u>Rehabilitation Counseling Bulletin</u>, <u>10</u>(3), 108-111.

Hagner, D., & Como, P. (1982). <u>Work stations in industry</u>. Menomonie, WI: University of Wisconsin-Stout, Stout Vocational Rehabilitation Institute, Materials Development Center.

Harris, J. A. (1982). APTICOM: A computerized multiple aptitude testing instrument for cost and time effective vocational evaluation. <u>Vocational Evaluation and Work Adjustment Bulletin</u>, <u>15</u>(4), 161-162.

Himstreet, W. C., & Baty, W. M. (1984). <u>Business communications: Seventh edition</u>. Boston, MA: Kent Publishing Company.

Leland, M., & Rice, B. D. (1982). Prescriptive vocational evaluation. In B. Bolton, Ed.), <u>Vocational adjustment of disabled persons</u> (pp. 71-91). Baltimore, MD: University Park Press.

Matarazzo, J. D. (1983). Computerized psychological testing (editorial). <u>Science</u>, <u>221</u>(4608).

Matheson, L. N. (1984). <u>Work capacity evaluation: Interdisciplinary approach to industrial rehabilitation</u>. Anaheim, CA: Employment and Rehabilitation Institute of California.

Matheson, L. N. (1985). <u>Work capacity evaluation: Interdisciplinary approach to industrial rehabilitation</u>. Two-day training workshop held in Buena Park, California.

McCray, P. M. (1982). <u>Vocational evaluation and assessment in school settings</u>. Menomonie, WI: University of Wisconsin-Stout, Stout Vocational Rehabilitation Institute, Research and Training Center.

McDaniel, R. S. (1972). Alabama rehabilitation counselors' attitudes about vocational evaluation: A consumer's opinion (unpublished study). Auburn, AL: Auburn University.

Miller, J. H., & Alfano, A. M. (1974). The efficacy of Tennessee rehabilitation facilities: A counselor critique. Vocational Evaluation and Work Adjustment Bulletin. 7(1), 31-37.

Nadolsky, J. (1985). Vocational evaluation: An experimental trend in vocational assessment. In C. Smith & R. Fry, (Eds), National forum on issues in vocational assessment (the issues papers) (pp. 1-9). Menomonie, WI: University of Wisconsin-Stout, Stout Vocational Rehabilitation Institute, Materials Development Center.

North Carolina Division of Vocational Rehabilitation Services. (1983). NC vocational rehabilitation client evaluations: A comprehensive review. Raleigh, NC: Department of Human Resources, Evaluation and Program Review Section.

Occupational Curriculum Laboratory. (1982). Vocational assessment of students with special needs: An implementation manual. Commerce, TX: East Texas State University.

Pell, K., Fry, R., & Langton, A. (1983). Vocational Evaluation and Work Adjustment Association Glossary. Menomonie, WI: University of Wisconsin-Stout, Stout Vocational Rehabilitation Institute, Materials Development Center.

Peterson, M. (1985). School-based vocational assessment: A comprehensive, developmental approach. In C. Smith & R. Fry (Eds.), National forum on issues in vocational assessment (the issues papers). Menomonie, WI: University of Wisconsin-Stout, Stout Vocational Rehabilitation Institute, Materials Development Center, 69-74.

Popham, E. L., Tilton, R. S., Jackson, J. H., & Hanna, J. M. (1983). Secretarial procedures and administration: Eighth edition. Cincinnati, OH: South-Western Publishing Company.

Rehabilitation Coordinators Incorporated. (1981). Vocational placement - A practical approach. Valley Forge, PA: Author.

Rice, B. D. (1972). Prescriptive vocational evaluation. Vocational Evaluation and Work Adjustment Bulletin, 5(1), 8-11.

Riley, B. J. (1980). A survey of job descriptions and salary ranges for vocational evaluators and work adjustment personnel in great plains region. Vocational Evaluation and Work Adjustment Bulletin, 13(4), 150-153.

Shainline, M. (1984). The use of microcomputers in the vocational assessment of high school students. Vocational Evaluation and Work Adjustment Bulletin, 17(1), 3-4.

Simmons, M. A. (1975). A survey of Georgia rehabilitation counselors' opinions about vocational evaluation reports. Vocational Evaluation and Work Adjustment Bulletin, 8(2), 24-28.

Sink, J. M., & Field, T. F. (1981). Vocational assessment planning and jobs. Athens, GA: VDARE Service Bureau.

Sink, J. M., & King, W. M. (1983). Evaluation services in the private sector. Vocational Evaluation and Work Adjustment Bulletin, 16(3), 96-99.

Smith, F. (1971). A rehabilitation counselor's model for work evaluation reports. Journal of Applied Rehabilitation Counseling, 2(4), 191-193.

Special Programs Unit. (1985). Challenge: A handbook for serving disadvantaged and handicapped students. Raleigh, NC: North Carolina Department of Public Instruction, Division of Vocational Education.

Tenth Institute on Rehabilitation Services. (1972). Vocational evaluation and work adjustment services in vocational rehabilitation. Menomonie, WI: University of Wisconsin-Stout, Department of Rehabilitation and Manpower Services, Materials Development Center.

Thomas, S. W. (1985). Preliminary results of the national vocational evaluator survey. VEWAA Newsletter, 12(4), 12-13.

VALPAR-SPECTIVE. (1975). ...The client report - comments and examples. Valpar-Spective, 1(4), 4-19.

Vocational Evaluation and Work Adjustment Association. (1984). MESA (Microcomputer Evaluation and Screening Instrument). Vocational Evaluation and Work Adjustment Bulletin, 17(2), 67-70.

Vocational Evaluation and Work Adjustment Association. (1975). Vocational evaluation project final report. Vocational Evaluation and Work Adjustment Bulletin, 8, (special edition).

Williams, D. M. (1975). A follow-up study on the relationship between work evaluators' recommendations and client placement. Menomonie, Wisconsin: University of Wisconsin-Stout, Stout Vocational Rehabilitation Institute.

APPENDICES

This final section is designed to illustrate the types of reports that are written in the various settings described throughout this book. Nine assessment/evaluation reports have been included to cover a wide range of examples. Inclusion of these reports is not an endorsement of their content, or of the service or product utilized, but a representation of the types of report formats and styles presently being written and used in the field.

Two reports have been included from traditional vocational rehabilitation settings: one short-term evaluation report from a division of vocational rehabilitation unit office, and a long-term evaluation report from a sheltered workshop.

Two assessment reports written for secondary school settings are also included: one conducted on a ninth grade student and the other on a twelfth grader, to illustrate the differences by grade level.

From the private-for-profit sector, two vocational evaluation reports have been incorporated as an example of a Social Security evaluation (determination of vocational capacity) and a Workers' Compensation evaluation (self-insured employer referral).

Due to the rapid growth in the use of computer-generated report writing, examples of reports from three work sample system developers have been included. These reports are all system dedicated documents that require data input from a particular set of instruments/sub-tests in order to obtain a printout.

APPENDIX A

VOCATIONAL REHABILITATION UNIT REPORT

The following report was based on a short-term (four hour) evaluation in a division of vocational rehabilitation unit office. This and other referrals are made by state agency vocational rehabilitation counselors to assist with eligibility determination for vocational rehabilitation services, assessment of vocational potential, and identification of possible rehabilitation, training, and employment options.

Report provided by:

Greenville Evaluation Program
Division of Vocational Rehabilitation Services
Greenville, North Carolina
Jim Warren, M.S., CVE, Vocational Evaluator
Jim Mullen, M.S., CVE, Evaluation Supervisor

DIVISION OF VOCATIONAL REHABILITATION

GREENVILLE EVALUATION PROGRAM

GREENVILLE UNIT OFFICE

EVALUATION REPORT

Confidential And Privileged Information Not To Be Used Against Client.

NAME: Anita Aid

DATE OF EVALUATION: 04/11/86

AGE: 26

DOB: 09/09/59

SEX: White Female

EDUCATION: Completed 10th Grade

HOME ADDRESS: 80 Decibels Drive, Greenville, NC

DISABILITY: Severe Hearing Impairment

REFERRED BY: Ricky Rehab

REASON FOR REFERRAL

Anita Aid was referred to the Greenville Evaluation Program to determine her level of vocational potential and possible areas of employment as they relate to her hearing impairment.

BACKGROUND INFORMATION

Anita Aid comes to the Evaluation Program with a disability of severe hearing impairment. Hearing impairment dates back to birth. She does use a hearing aid which is old and her discrimination levels are quite low.

Ms. Aid has past work experience which includes general maid and room cleanup work tasks, dishwashing, and some assembly line work in a cherry manufacturing plant when she was 21. She does have a valid North Carolina driver's license and owns her own vehicle. There appeared to be no other physical limitations with the exception of an expressed tenderness in the gall bladder area. Ms. Aid expresses her doctor has checked her gall bladder before for possible problems.

Ms. Aid lives with her husband and three children in the Greenville area and relies on her husband as a primary means of support. One of her children is in school and the other two children are two and four years of age. She would need some assistance with child care if employment was found. Ms. Aid does receive some payments from SSI in the amount of approximately $335 per month.

Anita Aid
Evaluation Report
Page two

GENERAL OBSERVATIONS

Anita Aid arrived promptly for her scheduled appointment at the Evaluation Center. She came dressed quite appropriately in a dress, dress shoes and sweater. She appeared to have well-kept hair and gave an overall appearance of practicing good personal hygiene. During the initial interview, Ms. Aid was observed to have some difficulty in comprehending statements made by this evaluator; however, she utilized her lipreading abilities to assist her. Ms. Aid did give the overall affect of a very personable individual with a motivated attitude. She made every effort to comprehend instructions given by this evaluator and did raise questions when in doubt. It was felt by this evaluator that overall communication levels were good considering her disability. Certain words were indistinguishable by Ms. Aid and had to be reworded for comprehension. Examples would be the words "ruin", "hobbies" and "preference". With the assistance of demonstrated and visual instruction and pantomime, it was quite easy to communicate with Ms. Aid. During the actual testing portion of the evaluation, Ms. Aid did have difficulty with the achievement testing due to her poor discrimination levels and low academic achievements. She also had difficulty with other evaluation instruments given to her which required reading beyond very simple sentence structure. She remained, however, motivated and showed good self-initiative in all the tasks assigned to her and demonstrated excellent concentration and effort.

TEST RESULTS

A. Revised Beta Examination, Second Edition (Beta II)

    Beta IQ: 93
    Percentile: 31st
    Intelligence Classification: Average

    Ms. Aid's performance on the Revised Beta Examination does indicate she is performing in the low average percentile when compared to her chronological age group, however suggests average intellectual functioning.

B. Wide Range Achievement Test-Revised

    Word Recognition: Standard Score - 54, Percentile - .2, GE - below 3
    Spelling: Standard Score - 56, Percentile - 9, GE - below 3
    Arithmetic: Standard Score - 56, Percentile - .4, GE - 3E

    Ms. Aid's performance on the achievement testing indicates she is functioning in the deficient range when compared to her chronological age group in all three academic areas. She was observed to have much difficulty in comprehending spelling words pronounced by this evaluator due to her hearing discrimination levels and also had difficulty in word pronunciation. She demonstrated math skills indicating potential for simple addition and subtraction of up to three-digit numbers.

Anita Aid
Evaluation Report
Page three

C. Reading-Free Vocational Interest Inventory

   Above Average Interests: Materials Handling
                                       Building Trades
                                       Clerical
                                       Housekeeping

   Below Average Interests: Personal Service
                                       Food Service
                                     Patient Care
                                     Laundry Service

Ms. Aid expressed to this evaluator an interest in working with her hands. Her high tested interest in materials handling and building trades as well as housekeeping activities shows good correlation with this expressed general interest area.

D. Sample Job Application Form

Ms. Aid's performance on completing a sample job application form indicates several deficits. She left much of the application form blank and indicated to this evaluator much difficulty in comprehending questions asked on the form. She obviously was having difficulty with the reading level of the application form. She could not remember the names and addresses of former employers and also did not know the names of any references she could give for a perspective employer. The section under physical record was left completely blank. She obviously needs some assistance and improvement in her ability to complete a sample job application form.

E. Minnesota Spatial Relations Test-Revised Edition - a performance test developed to assess an individual's perception of spatial relations and rapid manipulation of three-dimensional objects.

Time Score: 340 seconds
Standard Score: 116

Percentile: 90
Norms Used: Industrial Workers

Percentile: 80
Norms Used: Machine Trades

Error Score: 0

Ms. Aid's performance on the Spatial Relations Test indicates she is functioning in an above average percentile ranking when compared to the norm group consisting of males involved in machine trades programs and coursework. She also demonstrated above average ability when compared

Anita Aid
Evaluation Report
Page four

      with employed tool and dye makers, assemblers, punch-press operators, janitors, maintenance and repair personnel. Her error score of 0 indicates that she made no errors during the administration of this test and suggests a very organized and persistent individual. Observations during this work sample suggest to this evaluator that Ms. Aid shows good concentration and demonstrates good skills for tasks which would involve spatial relations aptitudes.

F. Purdue Pegboard - assesses gross movements of the hands and arms and "fingertip" dexterity.

   Norm Group: Female Hourly Production Workers

      Right Hand: Raw Score - 21
                  Percentile - 98

      Left Hand: Raw Score - 20
                 Percentile - 97

      Both Hands: Raw Score - 15
                  Percentile - 75

      Right + Left + Both: Raw Score - 56
                            Percentile - 95

      Assembly: Raw Score - 51
               Percentile - 98

   All scores measured by the Purdue Pegboard indicate above average potential for utilization of gross movements of the hands, arms and fingertips when compared to female hourly production workers.

G. Valpar Component Work Sample #8 - Simulated Assembly - designed to measure a person's ability to work at an assembly line task requiring repetitive physical manipulation, and to evaluate a person's bilateral use of the upper extremities.

   Number of Correct Assemblies: 317

   Percentile: 75-80
   Norm Group: Congenitally Deaf
   MTM Percent: 100-105

   Ms. Aid's performance on this work sample when compared to the norm group composed of congenitally deaf indicates an above average ability for this type of task. She also demonstrates competitive ability when compared to her Method-Time-Measurement Percent. Normally, a score of 100 on the MTM Percent would indicate an average level for competitive entry level skills for jobs requiring this type of task.

Anita Aid
Evaluation Report
Page five

H. Valpar Component Work Sample #9 - Whole Body Range of Motion - is a non-medical measure of the ability of a person to utilize gross bodily movements of the trunk, arms, hands, legs and fingers as they relate to physical capacities to perform job tasks.

    Time: 969 seconds
    Norm Group: Congenitally Deaf
    Percentile: 85-90
    MTM Percent: 130-135

    Ms. Aid's performance on the Whole Body Range of Motion Work Sample again indicates above average abilities when compared to a congenitally deaf norm group and to a Method-Time-Measurement scale. Her performance would indicate competitive ability for utilizing the whole body range of motion. She expressed to this evaluator no physical limitations during this administration and working from positions above one's head, bending at the waist and stooping. She was observed to cough several times during this work sample, however, and commented on her attempts to stop smoking. Her coughing was noted throughout the remainder of the evaluation session.

I. Bennett Hand-Tool Dexterity Test - constructed to provide a measure of proficiency in using ordinary mechanics tools.

    Time: 7 minutes, 19 seconds
    Norms Used: Employees and Applicants in a Manufacturing Company
    Percentile: 90th

    Ms. Aid's performance on the Hand-Tool Dexterity Test suggests above average ability when compared to employees and applicants in a manufacturing company. She did appear to be motivated during this work sample, however worked somewhat awkwardly with tools.

SUMMARY

Ms. Aid is a 26 year old white female who has completed her evaluation at the Greenville Evaluation Program. During this brief assessment period, Ms. Aid did demonstrate many deficits in her discrimination levels and comprehension levels as far as communication skills are concerned. She did, however, compensate for this by her personable attitude, motivation and self-initiative to participate in the evaluation. She demonstrated an excellent effort for attempting comprehension of all instructions given to her and her overall affect was that of an enjoyable individual. Ms. Aid's performance during the evaluation indicated competitive ability for physical tasks involving whole body range of motion including working above one's head, bending at the waist and stooping positions. She demonstrated a competitive ability for assembly type tasks as well as fine finger dexterity tasks. Ms. Aid also demonstrated above average ability for spatial visualization and a competitive rate of manipulation for three-dimensional objects. She demonstrated deficits in her achievement skills and severe deficits

Anita Aid
Evaluation Report
Page six

in her ability to complete a sample job application form. Her ability to work with hand tools appeared to be competitive when compared to employees and applicants in a manufacturing company. Ms. Aid's Beta IQ suggests she is functioning in the average range.

Ms. Aid's interest inventory suggests four possible areas for career exploration for interest. The materals handling, building trades, clerical and housekeeping areas were high areas of interest for her. Her expressed interest was to work with her hands. This shows good correlation with materials handling positions, building trades and housekeeping work. General clerical tasks related to filing activities or possibly sorting would also be feasible for her. Due to Ms. Aid's low achievement levels, general clerical work may involve reading or arithmetic skills which would seem unfeasible for her.

RECOMMENDATIONS

1. Ms. Aid demonstrates the potential for competitive work on the semi-skilled level. Factory work related to general production labor, assembly tasks involving gross or fine finger dexterity, as well as general inspection activities appear to be realistic vocational goals. Ms. Aid should also be able to handle housekeeping tasks involving janitorial skills and cleaning duties. Trade work utilizing tools is also feasible.

2. An on-the-job training contract may be helpful in establishing a skill training time period and may help in establishing an employee/employer relationship with the assistance of the counselor for the purpose of clear communication. While Ms. Aid does demonstrate the ability to accept responsibility, supervision will be needed to assist her in communication.

3. The Rehabilitation Engineer may be a useful resource in providing insight into job modification needs. Due to Ms. Aid's hearing impairment, she may need signaling devices to alert her to work breaks, production changes or time frames necessary in production work.

4. Ms. Aid would also appear to need job seeking skills development. She does have deficits in her ability to complete a sample job application form and may need coaching or assistance with communication in an initial interview.

5. A request for past medical records in regard to Ms. Aid's stated medical history of gall bladder problems may provide insight into any work related deficits. A general physical exam may also be helpful in assessing a persistent cough noted throughout this evaluation. (Client states history of tobacco abuse.)

6. Guidance and counseling into possible child care problems and alternatives for dealing with this would also be helpful in preparing Ms. Aid for on-the-job training or direct placement.

Jim Warren, MS, CVE No. 230
Vocational Evaluator

JW:pfd

APPENDIX B

SHELTERED WORKSHOP REPORT

The following report was based on a long-term vocational evaluation (30-day) that utilized production areas within a sheltered workshop setting for the bulk of the assessment. Rather than relating to immediate employment options, the report addresses the client's need for work adjustment services prior to job placement.

Report provided by:

Vocational Trades of Alamance and Caswell Counties
Burlington, North Carolina
Constance M. White, M.S., CVE, Vocational Evaluator

Vocational Trades
ALAMANCE-CASWELL AREA MENTAL
HEALTH/MENTAL RETARDATION AND
SUBSTANCE ABUSE AUTHORITY

NORTH CAROLINA DIVISION OF
MENTAL HEALTH/MENTAL RETARDATION
AND SUBSTANCE ABUSE SERVICES

CLIENT: RECORD NUMBER:

Age: 26   Date of Birth:

V.R. Number: V.R. Counselor:

Evaluator: Constance M. White   Date:

Evaluation Period:

BACKGROUND INFORMATION:

_____ was referred to VTA for evaluation of his vocational assets and liabilities to help determine his vocational potential as well as appropriate vocational goals.

Mr. _____ has a primary diagnosis of Bipolar Disorder, mixed and currently resides at Wesley Hall. He has been hospitalized three times in the past for mental illness, with the most recent being in May of 1984. Mr. _____ did attend VTA from 8/84 to 9/84 and evaluation results suggested "a lack of motivation" which contributed to poor work habits, productivity and quality. Also noted were his poor interpersonal skills. At this time, involvement at VTA was not found to be appropriate and Mr. _____ was referred to the Mental Health Center, Adult Day Program. Due to significant gains made in problem areas while in Day Treatment, referral to VTA was deemed appropriate.

Mr. _____ completed twelfth grade and has held several entry level jobs in the past, including restaurant worker and construction worker. He wears glasses and indicated that he used to have a slight hearing loss. A medical exam dated 1/23/86 indicated no physical problems.

General Observations:

During the pre-entry tour and interview, Mr. _____ presented as a moderately obese, well dressed and groomed male who was rather solemn. He stated that he was very interested in re-entering the program, and he was aware of reasons he was terminated before. Mr. _____ stated that it is time to get his life in order and he is working toward self-sufficiency.

During the intake interview, Mr. _____ did once again appear to be solemn, but did appear motivated. He answered all interview questions appropriately and accurately and gave the impression of an individual with above average intellectual ability.

During his evaluation, Mr. _____ was placed in several production areas and one service area (food service). This evaluator noted that Mr. _____ liked very structured work settings and tended to resist change. It was very obvious that he preferred to work alone and be responsible for his own work versus performing work as part of a team effort. This was

Form AP 1-03-85 (Rev.)

ADMISSION ASSESSMENT/
VOCATIONAL EVALUATION

CLIENT: _____   RECORD NUMBER: _____

especially apparent in food service, where his instructor noted him to be arrogant and uncooperative. He was very quiet and had very little interaction with his peers.

As far as his work quality was concerned, most instructors indicated that he produced good work. In the food service area however, Mr. _____'s work quality was noted to be below average on nearly every task.

As far as work quantity was concerned, Mr. _____ produced at a much higher level than the 11% competitive industrial standards he achieved during his previous evaluation. On production tasks, he averaged producing at 34% competitive industrial standards. The following information reflects his performance in all work areas:

Tasks	Quality/Quantity
Assemble power blocks (aluminum)	Good/36% CIS*
Assemble power blocks (copper)	Good/36% CIS*
Measure and cut 6-inch aluminum strips	Good/39% CIS*
Assemble total M 400 seal beam lamp	Good/24% CIS*
Tie knot into wires 1-inch from end	Good/40% CIS*
Heat seal plastic bag	Good/22% CIS*
Brush grease on valve body O ring	Good/19% CIS*
Insert ring into stem of pressure gauge--insert into valve body and secure with lock spring	Good/35% CIS*
Food Service	Below average on all tasks performed

*Competitive Industrial Standards

While attendance and punctuality were noted to be problems during his last evaluation, this was certainly not true during this evaluation period. Mr. _____ attended thirty consecutive days and was very conscientious about informing this evaluator about Mental Health Center appointments. He asked this evaluator several times about his performance, and stated that he wanted to do well.

Several instructors did note that Mr. _____ had difficulty accepting criticism and became easily frustrated. This did appear to be mainly related to the type of task he was performing. He had the most difficulty in the food service area, where he indicated that his instructor was not telling him how to perform tasks, just what to do. If his work was very structured and he knew what was expected of him at all times, Mr. _____ demonstrated very good work abilities. When decision making and initiative was required, he had a very difficult time.

Overall, this evaluator found Mr. _____ to be an individual who is very interested in making changes in his life. As indicated before, Mr. _____ questioned this evaluator several times about his overall performance, and stated that he wanted to do well. Mr. _____ has made

Form AP 1-03-85 (Rev.)   ADMISSION ASSESSMENT/
                                                    VOCATIONAL EVALUATION

CLIENT: RECORD NUMBER:

numerous significant gains since his last evaluation and is very motivated toward achieving self-sufficiency.

TEST RESULTS:

1. Academics: On the Peabody Individual Achievement Test (PIAT), Mr. _____ achieved above the 12.9 grade equivalent on mathematics, reading recognition and reading comprehension. When compared to recent high school graduates, percentile scores fell within the above average range. Results suggest that he has potential for college level training.
2. Interests: Results of the Career Occupational Preference System (COPS) suggested high interest in consumer economics (textiles and food service), skilled technology and skilled science occupations. Mr. _____ did not express any vocational preferences.
3. Direction Following Skills: Results of the Personnel Test for Industry--Oral Directions Test (PTI--ODT) suggested that Mr. _____ possesses abilities to follow complex, conditional oral directions. His scores suggested skills at the 75th percentile when compared with competitive workers.
4. Work Samples: On the Valpar Independent Problem Solving, Mr. _____ demonstrated above average abilities to perform work tasks requiring visual comparison and proper selection of a series of abstract designs. On Multi-Level Sorting, he demonstrated below average ability to make decisions while performing work tasks requiring physical manipulation and visual discrimination. This evaluator noted that Mr. _____ appeared to be more motivated during the first work sample, probably because this activity was much more challenging to him.

SUMMARY AND RECOMMENDATIONS:

Based on observations of work behaviors, instructor reports, test results and production information, Mr. _____ appears to have the following vocational assets:

1. Excellent attendance and punctuality;
2. Good physical condition;
3. Good work quality;
4. Good supervisor relations;
5. Good job tolerance;
6. High motivation to pursue competitive employment;
7. Appropriate grooming and dress;
8. Good learning ability for simple and complex tasks;
9. Above average academic skills.

Mr. _____ appears to have the following vocational liabilities:

1. Limited social relationships and peer interaction;
2. Productivity below competitive standards (34%);
3. Lack of transportation;
4. Limited ability to handle stress/low frustration tolerance.

Form AP 1-03-85 (Rev.)

ADMISSION ASSESSMENT/
VOCATIONAL EVALUATION

CLIENT: RECORD NUMBER:

When comparing results of this evaluation to results of Mr. _____'s previous evaluation, it is evident that significant gains have been made in many problem areas. Of utmost importance is Mr. _____'s motivation toward eventually achieving self-sufficiency. He is very intent on continuing work on his problem areas. For these reasons, this evaluator recommends a period of work adjustment training with a goal of competitive employment so that he can have the opportunity to sharpen his work skills. Mr. _____ did not indicate any specific vocational interest areas, but does seem to be interested in jobs which are structured where he is allowed to work primarily alone. Examples of jobs which may eventually be appropriate for him include: PARTS CLERK, (DOT222.367-042; INVENTORY CLERK, (DOT222.387-026); QUALITY-CONTROL CHECKER, (DOT789.387-010); and METER READER (DOT209.567-010). As Mr. _____ has very high academic skills it also needs to be noted that he may eventually be a good candidate for vocational training at the community college level.

Constance M. White
Constance M. White, M.S., C.V.E.
Vocational Evaluator

Dict: 4/9/86   Trans: 4/16/86 VS

Form AP 1-03-85 (Rev.)   ADMISSION ASSESSMENT/
                                                  VOCATIONAL EVALUATION

APPENDIX C

NINTH GRADE STUDENT REPORT

This report was based on a four day vocational assessment of a ninth grade student referred by a special education teacher. Recommendations focus primarily on preparation for and placement in vocational classes, and the necessary curriculum and instructional modifications.

Report provided by:

Northwestern Regional Vocational Assessment Center
Stephens City, Virginia
Frances G. Smith, CVE, Vocational Assessment Coordinator

Northwestern Regional Vocational Assessment Center
Rt. 11 Box 236
Stephens City, VA 22655

VOCATIONAL ASSESSMENT REPORT

Name: John Edward Smith   Date of Report: 04-15-86

ID Number: 079   Date of Birth: 05-03-70

Referring Division: Frederick County   Social Security #:none

Contact Person: G. Williams   Dates of Assessment: 01-06-86,

Home School: James Wood High School-   01-07-86, 01-08-86 and 03-17-86

  Amherst Campus

I. Referral Information and General Description:

   John was referred for an assessment of vocational potential and
occupational preferences by Frederick County Public Schools. John was a
15 year old, 9th grade student. In particular, the referral source
requested specific career information that addressed John's potential in
the reported interest areas of: general vocational abilities.
   During the initial interview, John stated that at present he was
enrolled in the Wood Technology vocational class. Previous vocational
classes included the Wood Technology vocational class in the 8th grade.
Past work experience was noted as rebuilding motors and working on Pullen
trucks with "Athey's Pullen Team" Also indicated was working at Big A's
Auto Parts as a stock helper and general helper. When asked to name a
positive characteristic he could offer an employer John replied, "I'm on
time". The student was cooperative with initial interview procedures.
   In addition, referral information and a talk with John indicated no
physical limitations or medications.

Vocational Interests

EXPRESSED VOCATIONAL INTERESTS
    Auto mechanics and carpentry.

CASE - CAREER ASSESSMENT SURVEY EXPLORATION
    An occupational interest inventory of 156 careers and developed
around the 13 career clusters utilized in the Occupational Outlook
Handbook. John identified the top interest cluster areas as
mechanics-repairs, agriculture, construction and industrial-manufacturing

Job Seeking/ Keeping Skills:

John expressed an average understanding of job seeking skills. He displayed difficulty in completing a job application as evidenced by numerous spelling and grammar errors. Future assistance may be helpful in this area.

Achievement Data:
Results on the referred achievement test, WRAT (04-19-85), were as follows:

Area	Grade	SS	Percentile
Reading	3.6	70	2
Spelling	3.0	65	1
Math	3.3	69	2

THE LEARNING STYLES INVENTORY
A listing of forty-five statements asking an individual's response to preferred learning styles. The instrument is divided into three main areas: information gathering/ receiving, social work conditions, and expressiveness preference. John's major learning style preferences were identified as auditory language, auditory numerical, social individual and social group.

Psychometric Tests:

THE PERSONNEL TEST FOR INDUSTRY- ORAL DIRECTIONS TEST was administered to assess the student's general ability to follow oral directions. Performance was at the 50th percentile in comparison to the vocational evaluation clients norm group. John obtained a 23 out of a possible 39 score.

THE PENNSYLVANIA BI- MANUAL WORKSAMPLE DEXTERITY TEST was administered to assess the student's combined finger dexterity of both hands, gross movements of both arms, eye-hand coordination and bi- manual coordination. Performance was at the 2.3 percentile in comparison to male and female high school students suggestive of the low employable range.

THE BENNETT MECHANICAL COMPREHENSION TEST was administered to assess the student's general ability to understand physical and mechanical principles of practical situations. Performance was at the 35th percentile in comparison to 11th grade technical high school students norm group.

THE BENNETT HAND- TOOL DEXTERITY TEST was administered to assess the student's manipulative skill's relative to mechanical occupations. Performance was at the 90th percentile in comparison to boys at a vocational high school norm group.

THE DVORINE COLOR VISION TEST was administered to assess the student's general ability for color discrimination. John scored within the normal range.

HAND DOMINANCE: Left____   Right__x__

Work Sample Performance:

Work samples from the VALPAR Component Work Sample Series (VCWS) were admininstered to assess certain physical and vocational abilities. John completed the following work samples:

VCWS #8, SIMULATED ASSEMBLY, measure's a person's ability to work at an assembly task requiring repetitive, physical manipulation and evaluates the bilateral use of upper extremities. MTM performance was at 85 percent for time and quality.

VCWS #9, WHOLE BODY RANGE OF MOTION, measure's a person's agility of gross body movements with the trunk, arms, hands, legs and fingers as they relate to functional ability to perform job tasks. MTM performance was at 135 percent for time and quality.

VCWS #11, EYE-HAND-FOOT COORDINATION, measure's a person's ability to use their eyes, hands and feet simultaneously and in a coordinated manner. MTM performance was at 140 percent for time and 65 percent for quality.

VCWS #16, DRAFTING, measure's a person's potential to compete in an entry level position requiring basic drafting skills. Work activities explored include: simple measuring, line perception, determining scaled dimensions, drawing schematics and diagrams, freehand drawing and interpreting blueprints. MTM performance was as follows:

Measuring- MTM performance was at 5 percent for quality.

Selected SAM- Skills Assessment Modules were administered to provide hands- on career exploration. All percentile scores were compared against average high school students. John completed the following modules:

SAM-RULER READING, assesses the student's ability to accurately measure and read a ruler to the nearest sixteenth of an inch. Performance was at the 32nd quality percentile. (Average)

Work samples were administered from the VIEWS- Vocational Information and Evaluation Work Samples System to assess general worker factors and the student's ability to perform in the related worker skill groups. Norm ratings are compared against mentally retarded persons and performance is rated by a high to low scale (3-2-1). John completed the following work samples:

NUT WEIGHING, measure's a person's ability to distinguish the need to add or remove nuts from a tray in order to align a marker to a specified weight setting on a scale. John achieved a 3 rating for time and a 1 rating for quality.

VALVE DISASSEMBLY, measure's a person's ability to disassemble an eight-part unit using a wrench and screwdriver, and to sort the parts properly. John achieved a 3 rating for time and a 1 rating for quality.

VALVE ASSEMBLY, measure's a person's ability to assemble an eight- part unit using a wrench and screwdriver and to sort the different parts properly. John achieved a 3 rating for time and a 3 rating for quality.

CIRCUIT BOARD ASSEMBLY, measure's a person's ability to complete a sixteen- part assembly utilizing a color- coded diagram. John achieved a 3 rating for time and a 3 rating for quality.

Results from MODAPT pre-determined time standards were supportive of an average time production standard= 50.75%.

Selected work samples were administered to allow hands- on career exploration and evaluation of related work criteria. The student achieved successful performance in the following areas:
(A= ASSET, L= LIMITATION)

ENGINE SERVICE (Singer #14)
A   removing flywheel correctly
A   setting and adjusting breaker point gap to .030", .020"
A   adjusting and setting spark plug gap to .030", .040
A   appropriate use of hand tools
A   flywheel torqued to 200 inch/lbs.
A   spark plug torqued to 175 inch/lbs.
A   cylinder head bolts torqued to 100 inch/ lbs.
A   flywheel hub recessed with index lugs
A   drains and changes oil without making a mess
A   maintains a clean and orderly work area
A   adheres to necessary safety precautions
A   correct disassembly of engine parts
A   correct reassembly of engine parts
A   testing for compression

PACKAGING AND MATERIALS HANDLING   (Singer #23)
A   assembling cardboard cartons correctly
A   following packing orders to obtain correct materials
A   placing correct number of items in each package
A   banding boxes according to directions
A   wrapping and packaging items securely
A   labeling boxes in legible print
A   correct use of hand tools
A   correct lifting method applied
A   moving weighted boxes by hand and hand truck
A   adhering to needed safety precautions
A   maintaining a clean and orderly work area

CARPENTER (Choice #81)
A   grouping lumber correctly according to length
A   marking correct lumber measurements
L   recording lumber measurements on blueprint
L   correctly completing lumber computations on blueprint
L   cutting lines squarely
A   adhering to safety precautions
A   correct use of hand tools
A   drawing lines squarely on lumber
A   measuring within a 1/4" tolerance
A   measuring within a 1/8" tolerance
A   centering guidelines
A   positioning plates and studs correctly on subfloor
L   correct placement and nailing of nails
A   correct wall plumb technique

A maintaining a clean work area

ELECTRICIAN (Choice #83)
A correctly testing circuit breaker with tester
L correctly measuring cable lengths
L correctly recording cable lengths on blueprint
A making correct cable runs between electrical boxes
L marking and extending correct inches of cable into electrical boxes
A marking and stripping insulation
A correct use of hand tools
A adherance of safety precautions
L correct connection of wires within electrical boxes
L screwing wire connections at a clockwise turn
A correct installation of electrical box interior and exterior parts
A wiring circuit breaker
A wired light on
A correct disassembly of unit, tools returned to appropriate place
A maintained a clean and orderly work area

4 CYCLE SMALL ENGINE DISASSEMBLE/ ASSEMBLE
   correct disassembly and re-assembly of:
A a. flywheel
A b. carburator
A c. cylinder head cover
A d. crankcase cover
A e. blower housing
A f. oil splash gear
A g. governor blade
A h. flywheel screen
A i. cylinder head
A j. muffler
A k. crankcase breather
L correct recognition of parts
L correct placement of parts into designated compartments
A correct use of hand tools
A organized work method and planning ability
A followed written manual instructions

Summary, Conclusions and Recommendations:

    John participated in approximately 20 hours of group and individualized assessment and work sample completion. The work samples that were of most interest to John were in the occupational areas of mechanics, carpentry and electrician.

VOCATIONAL ASSETS:
   motivated on task
   demonstrated iniative on task
   followed established safety rules and procedures
   demonstrated unimpaired whole body range of motion
   demonstrated unimpaired eye-hand-foot coordination
   followed a simple diagram
   used a simple model as work guide
   demonstrated unimpaired manual dexterity
   demonstrated unimpaired eye hand coordination
   ability to improve work speed with task repetition
   ability to improve work quality with task repetition

measuring within a 1/8" tolerance
appropriate use of hand tools

VOCATIONAL NEEDS:
limited numerical ability to complete mathematical computations (ie; working with decimals and fractions)
low reading grade level restricted use of written instructions
reading a ruler within 1/16" tolerance
mechanical comprehension skills
following 3-4 step oral directions
effectively completing job applications
work production speed
following complex diagrammatic instructions

The results of this assessment appear supportive of this student's final tested interest areas of mechanics, carpentry and electrician. Scores on related dexterity and manipulative tasks were in the competetive ranges and supported John's stated familiarity with these related tasks. In the mechanical areas, although tests measuring comprehension and mechanical conceptualizing skills did not reach high percentiles, his ease with the hands-on activities compensated well for these limitations. It should be noted that at the time of this assessment, the evaluator did not have the luxury of providing this student with the taped version of the Bennett Mechanical Comprehension Test. Re-administration of this taped version of the test may have yielded much higher scores.

Areas of concern noted on tasks appeared to relate most to John's difficulty with fine measuring tolerances, converting fractions to decimal equivalents, following 3-4 step oral instructions and work production speed. Modifications to the work environment included providing instruction primarily through visual means, audio-visual means and assisting with numerical functions.

John's approach to the assessment was displayed as positive. He maintained high work motivation throughout the assessment period. A careful work approach was noted, and may account for his lower work production time scores.

With consideration of this student's past vocational experiences, maintained tested interest and ability to work with related tasks, future vocational programming should be successful in his expressed areas.

RECOMMENDATIONS

Short Term:

1. Vocational counseling/ exploration to assist John with future career interests and directions.

2. Instruction in math skills to enhance fine measuring skills, working with decimals and fractions and using blueprints.

3. Instruction in reading skills to enhance reading vocational terms, blueprints, work orders, etc.

4. Utilization of CRI materials in Auto Mechanics and Residential Construction to enhance John's acquistion of vocational terminology.

5. Consider providing vocational instruction in ways which can complement John's preferred learning styles.

6. Consider placement in the Agricultural Science & Mechanics I vocational class (10th grade) to enhance John's mechanical skills and interests.

Long Term:

1. Consideration for placement in the Auto Mechanics I vocational class (11th grade). The instructor should be aware of John's reading level, as John would have difficulty reading a textbook. Begin working on the competencies outlined in the Appendix. This list is not all inclusive, but is meant as a guide for the instructor, and to allow John to achieve as many competencies as possible.

The following alterations in John's program are recommended to ensure that he has the best chance to succeed in the program.

   a. Tests given as a hands-on experience or read to John.
   b. Support services to assist John with written textbook work.
   c. Tape record or verbally provide written instruction

2. Consideration for placement in the Building Trades I vocational class (11th grade). The instructor should be aware of the recommended alterations in John's program. Begin working on the competencies as outlined in the Appendix. Consider placement in the Wood Technology II vocational class (10th grade) to enhance skill level and interest in the structural areas.

4. Consideration for placement in the Electricity/ Electronics Technology vocational program (11th grade). The instructor should be aware of the recommended alterations in John's program. Begin working on the competencies as outlined in the Appendix.

Examples of jobs John might be able to obtain upon successful completion of the related vocational programs:

1. Auto Mechanic Helper 620.684-014
2. Auto Mechanic Apprentice 620.261-012
3. Carpenter Apprentice 860.381-026
4. Form Builder 860.361-046
5. Construction Worker I 869. 664-014
5. Carpenter, Rough 860. 381-042
6. Dry- Wall Applicator 842. 381-010

Frances G. Smith
Frances G. Smith, CVE
Vocational Evaluator

NORTHWESTERN REGIONAL VOCATIONAL ASSESSMENT CENTER

Work Behavior Rating Form

Name: John Edward Smith Date: 01-06-86, 01-07-86, 01-08-86
and 03-17-86

KEY

A - Vocational Asset   L - Vocational Limitation
U - Not Observed   NA - Not Applicable

BEHAVIORAL FACTORS   RATING

1. <u>Personal Appearance</u>

    Hygiene . . . .   A

    Grooming . . . .   A

    Dress . . . .   A

2. <u>Conformity to Rules and Regulations at Work</u>

    Attendance . . . .   A

    Punctuality . . . .   A

    Notification given when absent/late . . . .   U

3. <u>Conformity to Safety Rules and Regulations</u>

    General behavior . . . .   A

    Safety rules followed . . . .   A

4. <u>Reactions to Assigned Work</u>

    Distractability . . . .   A

    Attention span . . . .   A

    Reaction to unpleasant or repetitive tasks . . . .   A

    Personal complaints . . . .   A

    Reaction to change in work assignment . . . .   A

5. <u>Interpersonal Traits</u>

    Recognition/acceptance of supervisory authority . . . .   A

    Amount of tension aroused by close supervision . . . .   A

    Reaction to suggestions or constructive criticism . . . .   A

    Reaction to pressure from supervisor . . . .   A

    Request for assistance from supervisor . . . .   A

    Appropriate questions asked . . . .   A

6. Communication Skills   RATING

   Relates work needs to supervisors . . . . A

   He/she communicated his/her work needs to supervisors . . . . . . A

7. Initiative Factors

   Amount of supervision required after initial instruction
   period . . . . A

   Working without supervision . . . . A

   Independently return to work after breaks . . . . A

   Recognition of errors L

   Correction of errors . . . . A

   Maintenance of orderly work area . . . . A

8. Work Capability

   Steadiness or consistency of work . . . . A

   Stamina or eight-hour work capacity . . . . A

   Vitality of work energy . . . . A

9. Socialization

   Social skills in relations with co-workers . . . . A

   His/her social skills in relations to co-workers were
   appropriate . . . . A

   Other:

APPENDICES

Work Preferences: The student exhibited a preference toward working with the following activities during the assessment period.

	YES	NO	U
1. Activities involving things and objects.	X		
2. Activities involving business contact with people.	X		
3. Routine, concrete, organized activities.	X		
4. Working for the good of people (as in social welfare), or dealing with people and language in social situations.		X	
5. Increasing his prestige or obtaining the esteem of others.		X	
6. Activities involving people and the communication of ideas.	X		
7. Scientific or technical activities.	X		
8. Abstract or creative activities.			X
9. Non-social activities using processes, machines, techniques.	X		
10. Activities resulting in tangible, productive satisfaction.	X		

Working Conditions The student appeared capable of working under the following conditions. Ratings are the result of observations of work performance and discussions with the student concerning his/her interests.

	YES	NO	U
1. Inside (indoors)	X		
2. Outside (outdoors)	X		
3. Extremes of cold plus temperature changes.	X		
4. Extremes of heat plus temperature changes	X		
5. Wet and humid (extremes)	X		
6. Noise and vibration (extremes)	X		
7. Hazards, (mechanical, electrical, heights, etc.)	w/supervision		
8. Fumes, odors, toxic conditions, dust, poor ventilation discomforts effecting respiratory system.	X		

Physical Capacities: The student demonstrated potential and interest in performing the following physical activities.

	YES	NO	U
1. Lifting, carrying, pushing, pulling (strength):			
Sedentary work (lift max. of 10 lbs.; mostly sitting)			
Light work (lift max. of 20 lbs.; or much walking or standing; or many work movements while sitting)			
Medium work (lift max. of 50 lbs., often carry up to 25 lbs., and many work movements while sitting)	X		
Heavy work (lift max. of 100 lbs., often carry up to 80 lbs.)	possibly		
Very heavy work (lift over 100 lbs, often carry up to 80 lbs.)			
2. Climbing (agility); balancing (equilibrium)			
Stooping, kneeling, crouching, crawling (use of lower extremities and back muscles)	X		
Reaching, handling, fingering, feeling (use of upper extremities)	X		
3. Talking and hearing (as required on the job)		X	
4. Seeing (eyesight adequate for safety and for accuracy)	X		

AUTOMOTIVE MECHANICS

1. Steam clean engine.
2. Inspect exhaust system.
3. Replace exhaust manifold(s).
4. Replace muffler.
5. Remove and replace oil pump.
6. Remove and replace oil pans.
7. Replace tailpipe assemblies.
8. Lubricate universal joints.
9. Adjust headlights.
10. Clean, gap and test spark plugs.
11. Replace flasher units.
12. Replace starters.
13. Service or replace batteries, cables, and battery box.
14. Clean or replace fuel filter.
15. Remove and replace fuel pump.
16. Check coolant freezing point.
17. Check overflow tank.
18. Check coolant temperature.
19. Chemically clean and flush cooling system.
20. Inspect, adjust, or replace fan belts.
21. Remove and replace radiators.
22. Replace heater hoses.
23. Replace water pump.
24. Test and replace thermostat.
25. Replace shock absorbers and mounting.
26. Check manual steering gear fluid level.
27. Lubricate steering gear and linkage.
28. Adjust brakes.
29. Adjust parking brake linkage.
30. Bleed hydraulic brakes.
31. Inspect and replace brake pads (disc brakes).
32. Repair wheel cylinder.
33. Replace brake shoes.
34. Replace master cylinder.
35. Replace wheel cylinder.
36. Balance wheels and tires.
37. Lubricate ball joints.
38. Lubricate the front and rear suspension.

CARPENTRY

1. Bore holes with hand brace using augers and expansion bits.
2. Drill bore holes with the portable hand drill.
3. Bore holes with drill press.
4. Cut holes with keyhole saw.
5. Select proper hammer and drive various types and sizes of nails.
6. Set nails with nail set and apply wood filler.
7. Check and align installations for level and plumb with carpenter's level.
8. Identify actual sizes of milled lumber in relation to nominal sizes.
9. Identify defects and blemishes that affect durability and strength of lumber.
10. Stack and care for lumber.
11. Identify abbreviations commonly used in working with lumber.
12. Identify job safety requirements.
13. Use personal protective equipment.
14. Build saw horses.
15. Install floor joints.
16. Frame floor openings.
17. Install bridging between joints
18. Lay sub-floors.
19. Lay out a framing story pile.
20. Frame a wall opening.
21. Building corner posts.
22. Frame exterior walls.
23. Install diagonal bracking.
24. Align and brace a wall from corner to corner.
25. Frame and align partition wall.
26. Install dry-wall boards.
27. Install layment for pre-fabricated walls boards.
28. Install metal corners for dry-wall.
29. Install pre-fabricated panel and panel trim.
30. Apply prefinished hardboard.

ELECTRICITY

1. Identify tools.
2. Identify materials.
3. Wire doorbell and chime circuit.
4. Wire general lighting circuit.
5. Wire small appliance circuit.
6. Wire multiwire (common neutral) circuit.
7. Wire window air conditioner outlet.
8. Wire electric clothes dryer outlet.
9. Wire electric range outlet.
10. Wire ground fault interrupter circuit.
11. Split receptacle circuit.
12. Wire/install electric baseboard heat.
13. Wire/install smoke/fire detector.
14. Install low voltage lighting control system.
15. Select and install overcurrent devices.
16. Troubleshoot and repair non-operative or malfunctioning circuit.
17. Test for continuity.
18. Measure resistance.
19. Measure voltage.
20. Measure current.
21. Cut, ream, and thread conduit.
22. Bending conduit.
23. Installing conduit.
24. Pulling wire.
25. Calculating conduit size.
26. Bending tubing.
27. Installing tubing.
28. Check transformer nameplate for data.
29. Connect transformer for step down function (single phase).
30. Connect transformer for step up function (singe phase).
31. Parallel two single phase transformers.
32. Reverse direction of shaft rotation.
33. Connect to motor starter.
34. Connect dual voltage motor for operation.
35. Reverse direction of shaft rotation.
36. Connect to motor starter.
37. Wire a magnetic controller for automatic operation.
38. Wire a magnetic controller for manual operation (start/stop station).
39. Tool Safety.
40. Preventing electrical shock.

NORMATIVE DATA

1. MTM (Methods Time Measurement): On MTM scale, scores near the 100 percent level signify performance comparable to persons with entry level skills for jobs requiring that type of activity.

2. MODAPTS- (Modular Arrangement of Predetermined Time Standards): A predetermined time standard reflecting the time taken by an "average", experienced and trained worker in industry working at a normal pace.

3. SAM- Average High School Students: Representative of average vocationally bound, secondary students. All norms contain approximately 50 percent female and 50 percent male which average between 14-17 years of age.

4. Male and Female High School Students (PENNSYLVANIA BI-MANUAL). Based on the performance of 550 male and female students, ages 15 years and 0 months to 17 years and 11 months, in urban and suburban public and private schools of secondary level.

APPENDIX D

TWELFTH GRADE STUDENT REPORT

The following report was based on a 22 hour vocational assessment of a twelfth grade student referred by a multi-disciplinary team (resource room teacher, school psychologist, and social worker). The recommendations identify the student's adjustment needs and post-school employment options.

Report provided by:

Regional Vocational Assessment Center
University of Washington
Seattle, Washington
Megan Sheridan, M.S., Vocational Evaluator
Debra L. Kaplan, M.S., CRC, Vocational Evaluation Project Director

UNIVERSITY OF WASHINGTON
SEATTLE, WASHINGTON 98195

Child Development & Mental Retardation Center
Experimental Education Unit, WJ–10

Regional Vocational Assessment Center

VOCATIONAL EVALUATION REPORT

Name: Stone Peters   Evaluation Period: 10/28 - 10/31, 1985

Age: 17   Referral Source: Union Island High School

Disabling Condition: Behavioral Disability   Contact: Wanda Sabak

I. **Reason for Referral**

Stone Peters was referred by Union Island High School for an assessment of his vocational potential. Specific referral questions are as follows:

1. Does Stone possess acceptable social behavior for the work environment?

2. How will Stone handle himself when put under pressure on the job?

3. What would be realistic goals for Stone?

4. Would a community college vocational program be realistic for Stone or would an apprenticeship on the job program work better?

II. **Disabling Condition**

Referral information reports Stone's disabling condition as a behavioral disability. The referral information reports that Stone has an explosive temper. Despite this, he apparently has successfully worked for the School District on a maintenance crew. His employer was reportedly very pleased with his work. The referral information further reports that he was asked to leave his home, but has since returned with very specific rules he must follow.

III. **Impressions, Observations and Worker Characteristics**

Stone was punctual throughout most of the evaluation, but was absent the second day. He notified the evaluator about the absence the preceding day. He did not reveal a reason for the absence other than it related to his future.

Initially, he seemed quite resistant to the evaluation process. Negative and/or sarcastic comments about work samples and tests were frequent. Several times he made comments under his breath which seemed to be intended for the evaluator's hearing. He joked and laughed with another student throughout the first day, commenting to the evaluator that the two of them were "the worst." When confronted about his behavior he asked for specific examples and denied any unhappiness with going through the evaluation. After this he made fewer negative comments but maintained a flat affect and, with only one exception, reported that the work samples were only "alright." Joking and laughing with the other student continued, but less frequently.

During interactions with the evaluator he rarely smiled. When he did so it seemed to be an effort. For the most part, during both counseling and test administrations, he was fairly uncommunicative.

During the final two days of the evaluation, Stone seemed more interested in and cooperative with the process. He asked for feedback on his performance and reported that he enjoyed a work sample related to drafting. Throughout the evaluation the evaluator had joked that she hoped to find a task he would enjoy. When given the drafting work sample, he quipped, in a friendly voice, that she had finally found a test he liked. Stone also seemed more communicative during career exploration discussions. In particular, he seemed to open up more after the evaluator indicated she would personally research wages and availability of occupations of interest to him.

A final incident should also be noted. During lunch on the final day, Stone and other students apparently teased a young woman also participating in the evaluation. According to him she left the room because of this. By his report, he also left to look for her. This search caused him to be 15 minutes late. He seemed remorseful about the incident and indicated a desire to apologize. He subsequently did so. Notably, to the evaluator's knowledge, he was the only one of the group to do so.

IV. **Vocational Interests**

Expressed interest was in working as a mechanic or carpenter. During career exploration, Stone continued to express similar interests. He indicated particular interest in working as a mechanic, but expressed concern about wages and job availability. He indicated he wanted to earn enough to support a family, citing a minimum salary of $16,000 to $20,000 per year. Other possible occupational choices included drafting, mechanical drawing, and working as a fireman. He thought he might enjoy drafting or mechanical drawing but was concerned that these might be too sedentary. Stone reported that his father had worked as a fireman. He thought this might also be a possibility for him if other options did not work. He also expressed interest in architecture, but felt his dislike of and difficulty with math would limit him in this area.

Manifest interests were fairly consistent with expressed interests. When asked, Stone reported that he most enjoyed work samples related to inspecting, mechanics, electronics and drafting.

His profile on the California Occupational Preference System represented a fairly even distribution of scores. All scores but one fell in the average range. His lowest score was in the skilled science occupational cluster. His highest scores were in the skilled technology and professional arts occupational clusters. These scores are quite consistent with his expressed interest in mechanics, carpentry, drafting and architecture.

V. **Evaluation Results**

Psychometrics:

Bennett Mechanical Comprehension Test
75th %ile   Norm Group: 12th graders in an academic high school

This test is a measure of an individual's ability to recognize mechanical and physical factors which apply to practical situations. Stone's score suggests strength in mechanical reasoning.

Industrial Reading Test
95th %ile   Norm Group: students in programs in service occupations

This test measures the individual's ability to comprehend written technical material, and shows whether or not he/she has the necessary reading ability to make satisfactory progress in technical training. Stone's score indicates that he would have little difficulty reading material associated with a training program.

Revised Minnesota Paper Form Board Test
40th %ile   Norm Group: 12th grade New England boys

This test is a measure of spatial relations abilities. It measures an individual's ability to understand the interrelationships of parts of various kinds of assemblies, as well as the ability to utilize such pictorial representations of assemblies as blueprints, working drawings, etc. Two-dimensional spatial relations perception is an asset in such tasks as mechanics, drafting, graphic arts and engineering.

One should note that Stone completed only 44 of 64 problems in this test. He made no errors in the problems completed.

Raven Standard Progressive Matrices
75th %ile   Norm Group: age group

This nonverbal test of analytical reasoning measures an individual's immediate capacities for observation and clear thinking. Visual pattern recognition, visual attention and strong concentration are most important. The test is a good measure of mental strength and endurance on tasks requiring lengthy mental concentration.

Work Samples:

The work samples listed below are scored as follows:

1. A rating of 3 for speed or performance indicates that the student's performance falls into the interval between 61 and 99 percent of all those who took the sample.

2. A rating of 2 for speed or performance indicates that the student's performance falls into the interval between 40 and 60 percent of all those who took the sample.

3. A rating of 1 for speed or performance indicates that the student's performance falls into the interval between 1 and 39 percent of all those who took the sample.

On Valpar work samples, scores are recorded as an industrial standard called METHODS TIME MEASUREMENT (MTM). Scores near the 100 percent level signify performance comparable to persons with entry level skills for jobs requiring that type of activity. Scores above the 100 percent level signify better than entry level skills, while scores below suggest that some improvement would be required to acquire entry level proficiency.

JEVS #5: Sign Making
Time Rating: 1   Quality Rating: 2

On this work sample, the individual uses a ruler, marker, and letter stencils to create 3 signs. This work sample is a good indicator of whether or not an individual possesses basic skills in graphics.

Stone used fairly good planning and organization to perform this work sample. Errors in neatness and ruling were noted, however. Stone worked quite slowly on this task. This seemed largely attributable to off-task behavior. Much joking with other students and complaining about the activity were noted.

JEVS #12: Collating Leather Samples
Time Rating: 3   Quality Rating: 3

This work sample requires that an individual compare leather samples by color and texture to a sample of leather swatches that are bolted together. It requires fine color discrimination, textural discrimination and good bimanual coordination.

JEVS #30: Pipe and Union Assembly
Time Rating: 3   Quality Rating: 3

This work sample requires that an individual use two-dimensional diagrammatic instructions to complete a three-dimensional assembly of pipes and unions. It requires spatial relations perception and good bimanual coordination and dexterity.

Stone appeared to have little difficulty following the diagrammatic instructions. Initially he placed two t-joints incorrectly at the corners, but identified and corrected this mistake independently.

JEVS #31: Belt Assembly
Time Rating: 3   Quality Rating: 3

In this work sample a leather belt is disassembled and then all of the small geometric leather pieces are rejoined to assemble the belt. An individual must complete the work sample without committing any errors in order to receive a competitive quality score and he must complete the work sample in 19 minutes in order to reach competitive time levels.

Stone identified the reassembly process with no apparent difficulty. He reported average interest in this work sample, indicating that it was better than a paper and pencil test.

JEVS #36: Lock Assembly
Time Rating: 3   Quality Rating: 3

On this work sample, the evaluee disassembles and reassembles a lock without using any written or diagrammatic instructions. Because there are no instructions, strong attention to the task, especially during the disassembly section is important in order to remember how to reassemble the lock. Spatial form perception, visual memory and mechanical reasoning are especially important.

Stone demonstrated good planning and organization when he laid some of the parts on his work bench according to their order of placement in the lock. He subsequently reassembled the lock quickly. Three tests for correct function are used during this work sample. Ideally, these are performed at the end of the task just prior to screwing the top plate of the lock into place. Stone, however, screwed the plate into place prior to testing for function. When one part did not work correctly, he then needed to remove the top plate again. Once he did this he readily corrected his error.

JEVS #51: Nail and Screw Sorting
Time Rating: 3   Quality Rating: 3

On this work sample, the individual uses a ruler to measure and sort nails and screws. The individual must pay close attention to detail when measuring the objects to as little as 1/16 of an inch.

Stone demonstrated good motion economy when he measured one of each screw and nail, and sorted the rest to match. He reported that the work sample was "easy," but expressed no particular enthusiasm about the activity.

JEVS #53: Payroll Computation
Time Rating: 3   Quality Rating: 2

This work sample requires that an individual compute the payroll for 25 employees. There are 5 items which require computing overtime and written instructions for this type of computation accompany the work sample. The individual must be able to multiply and add in order to complete the task.

Much off-task behavior was noted during this work sample. Stone stated repeatedly that he hated math. He stopped midway through the work sample and said he could not do any more. When requested to complete it, however, he did so. Four errors in multiplication and one error in addition were noted.

JEVS #70: Pipe Assembly
Time Rating: 3   Quality Rating: 3

On this work sample, the evaluee assembles pipes from large to small. There are specific assembly rules to follow, and the evaluee must have strong skills in size discrimination, independent problem solving and bimanual dexterity.

Stone demonstrated excellent problem solving skills during this work sample. While he demonstrated a flat facial expression throughout the work sample and described it as "alright," Stone later reported that this was one of the more enjoyable activities of the assessment.

JEVS #90: Condensing Principle
Time Rating: 1   Quality Rating: 3

In this work sample, the evaluee uses a variety of drafting instruments including a t-square, triangles and a ruler to copy a blueprint of a condenser. The task requires extreme attention to detail and accuracy.

He worked with obvious care during this work sample. Stone reported that he had previously used all of the tools required in this activity. This was obvious by his performance. He did work slowly on the activity and this appeared largely attributable to much off-task behavior. He reported enjoyment of this work sample, but expressed concern that this type of work might be too sedentary.

VCWS #10: Tri-Level Measurement
Speed - 85% MTM   Accuracy - 150% MTM

This quality control work sample requires that the evaluee test machined parts to specific tolerances using three processes which include visual checking, jigs and precision measuring instruments such as a vernier caliper and a micrometer. The individual must use diagrammatic aides and extreme attention to detail. The evaluee also follows a specific process in order to complete the task with accuracy.

Stone demonstrated little difficulty learning the multiple steps involved in this work sample. With further practice one would expect that his speed might improve.

VCWS #12:   Soldering and Inspection
Section 1:   Speed - 50% MTM   Accuracy - 150% MTM
Section 2:   Speed - 125% MTM   Accuracy - 150% MTM
Section 3:   Speed - less than 5% MTM   Accuracy - 135% MTM
TOTAL: Speed - 60% MTM   Accuracy - 150% MTM

This work sample measures an individual's ability to complete tasks related to and including actual soldering. The evaluee uses wire cutters, strippers and needlenose pliers to complete a mechanical twist splice of wire and then solders the splice. This splice is then connected to a printed circuit board which is constructed by the evaluee.

Stone was quite dextrous in using the tools involved in this task. In particular, he demonstrated good control in using the soldering iron to apply solder. As may be noted, work speed was below industrial standards on two of the three sections. This would probably improve with practice. Stone described this activity as "too boring." Again, he felt the activity was too sedentary. He desired more active, mobile jobs.

VI. Summary and Recommendations

Stone Peters is a 17 year old 12th grader at Union Island High School. He is reportedly diagnosed as behaviorally disabled. The referral information reports that "his temper gets him in trouble." He apparently has worked for the School District, performing maintenance work. Feedback from the employer has been positive. Tested academic levels from 1983 were reported to range from the grade school to high school levels.

Resistance to the testing process was noted throughout much of the evaluation. Negative and/or sarcastic comments about tests and joking with and talking to other students during testing were noted. When confronted about his behavior, Stone was less vocal with his complaints but continued to present a flat affect and little enthusiasm toward the tests and work samples. On one occasion, he stopped work on a work sample, complaining in a sharp tone that he hated and worked poorly at that type of work. He also missed one day of the evaluation, citing an undisclosed reason that related to his future. As the evaluation progressed, Stone seemed somewhat more responsive to the process. He spoke fairly openly about vocational options and even expressed enjoyment of a work sample. During the teasing incident described earlier, he also displayed a sensitivity to another student's feelings not observed in other students participating in the evaluation.

Expressed vocational interest was in working in auto mechanics or carpentry. In both cases, he was concerned about wages and job availability. During career exploration, he continued to express similar interests, adding drafting, working as a fireman, and architecture to his list of interests. He was concerned that drafting might be too sedentary. Although he expressed a fairly lively interest in architecture, he felt his math skills were not adequate for the field. Both tested and manifest interests were fairly consistent with expressed interests.

Stone demonstrated several strengths during the evaluation. He was able to make fine color and texture discriminations, measure to a 1/16" tolerance and work within precise tolerances. He also learned multiple step procedures and demonstrated strengths in finger dexterity, manual dexterity, bimanual coordination and small hand tool usage. He used good planning and organization when performing most work samples as well. He was able to perform manual arithmetic computations such as multiplication and addition, but did not maintain accuracy on a work sample requiring this ability. On a graphics related task, which apparently engaged his interest, his work was quite neat, well planned and fell within very precise tolerances. On another graphics task he apparently disliked, neatness and precision were lacking. Strengths in comprehension of written technical material, mechanical comprehension, analytical reasoning, endurance for mentally rigorous tasks, independent problem solving and visual memory were noted. While Stone demonstrated strengths in spatial perception and form perception in applied situations, he scored in the low average range on a psychometric test that evaluated two-dimensional spatial perception. He learned new tasks easily with minimal verbal instruction. He also learned by means of written, demonstrated and diagrammatic instructions, as well as through the use of models. Throughout the evaluation he expressed a preference for learning and working with his hands.

Given the information contained in this report, recommendations are as follows:

1. One would hope that Stone's behavior and work habits in the work place would be different than those demonstrated during this evaluation. Favorable reports from his employer suggests this might be the case. If not, he will need to improve these as they will pose as barriers to successful education and employment. Certainly, work habits and work related behaviors should be addressed

during the remaining months of high school and thereafter as necessary. Initially, an individual with whom he has developed some rapport, might work with Stone in these areas. Reality based work adjustment counseling is suggested. The following work adjustment issues should be addressed:

a. **Increase On-Task Behavior** - Stone should be encouraged to work quietly in work situations requiring this behavior. This includes minimizing talking and joking with others. Setting a steady work pace should also be encouraged. Again, a reality based approach to increasing this behavior is suggested, emphasizing that employers find off-task behavior unacceptable.

b. **Improve Interactions with Supervisors** - Stone should be aware that the manner in which he interacts with others can affect his employability. In particular, an apparent lack of enthusiasm, complaints about assignments, and/or failure to comply with supervisor requests can all impact employability. Again, reality based work adjustment counseling addressing appropriate ways to interact with supervisors and deal with their requests and instructions is suggested. Prompt, constructive feedback regarding his interactions with others is also recommended. Consequences for his behavior should be well defined and enforced. In making this recommendation, the evaluator recognizes that Stone demonstrated a serious demeanor throughout the evaluation. One would hope that he could learn to demonstrate more positive, enthusiastic responses without compromising his basic manner.

c. **Improve Attendance** - One should note that Stone's absence the second day of the evaluation may have been an occurrence unique to the evaluation setting. In any case, he should be aware that employers expect regular attendance. When an absence must occur, prompt notification and statement of a valid excuse is usually required.

d. **Increase Frustration Tolerance** - At present, Stone seems to have a low frustration tolerance for apparently disliked and/or difficult tasks. This was evidenced by frequent complaints and even a work stoppage during such tasks. This could pose as a barrier to both post-secondary training and employment. Again, work adjustment counseling should address this issue. Therapeutic counseling, if not already occurring, might also help him to learn ways to deal with frustrating situations. Eastview Mental Health might be contacted for this purpose at 555-4367. Notably, Eastview Mental Health also periodically offers anger management groups. Given the referral source's report that Stone has temper outbursts, participation in such a group might also be considered.

2. Test results suggested that Stone might benefit from either formal or on-the-job post-secondary training. His preference for working with his hands indicates any training should have a strong practical emphasis. Good reading comprehension suggested he could handle community college or vocational technical school textbook material, if needed. He does appear to have deficits in math skills. This would probably make post-secondary training in drafting or architecture difficult since the former requires intermediate algebra and trigonometry, and the latter, calculus.

3. Stone does appear to have potential to train successfully in auto mechanics and related occupations, as well as in carpentry.

   a. Availability of auto mechanic's jobs varies according to setting, training and experience. Graduates of vocational technical school and community college training programs are considered to be journeymen. These people can get into training programs at automobile dealerships, starting at anywhere from about $5.00 to $8.50 per hour. Availability of such training positions varies according to individual dealerships. Persons working in the field contacted by the evaluator stressed that jobs can be found if the job seeker looks hard enough. As an individual gains skills and experience, pay increases. A BMW repair specialist reported that mechanics working on specialty imports can make $30,000 to $35,000 per year. Other more commonly quoted wages for working on mid-range priced cars were $12 to $15 per hour. Math deficits do not appear to be a problem in terms of admission to a training program. Because of computerized systems, math deficits might make learning to work with post 1982 cars more difficult. Notably, most community colleges and vocational technical school programs offer support services to individuals with skill deficits. If Stone encounters difficulty with coursework in a post secondary program, he might utilize such services. Programs to consider for auto mechanics include South Steed Community College (555-4356), contact: Dr. White (highly recommended by all repair shops contacted); Lake Crest Vocational Technical Institute (555-3411) (also specifically recommended by one contact); and Glover Hill Vocational Technical Institute (555-2321). Stone should be encouraged to investigate these programs. Interviews with instructors and tours are suggested.

    b. Carpentry jobs also appear to be available to the individual who makes an effort to find them. An individual apparently can train at a vocational technical school or community college, and then enter an apprenticeship program. He or she can also directly enter an apprenticeship program. In the latter case, the individual must find an employer who will hire him or her as a first year apprentice. The apprenticeship subsequently involves paid work with the employer and unpaid classroom work through the Carpenter's District Counsel (555-8425). According to the contact at the Carpenter's District Counsel, apprenticeship salary is 45% of journey level. Journey level salary is $17.32 per hour. The contact further stressed that community college and vocational technical school programs offer only "60 to 70 percent" of the training offered by their program. He also stressed that it is the only state approved apprenticeship program for carpentry. If Stone's interest in carpentry continues, he should be encouraged to contact this program.

4. Other training programs Stone might investigate include at Lake Crest Vocational Technical Institute (555-3271): auto body repair and refinishing, diesel maintenance and heavy equipment repair, motorcycle mechanics; at Glover Hill Vocational Technical Institute (555-2342): auto body repair and refinishing, office equipment service technician; and at South Steed Community College (555-5490): landscape design and construction, auto body building and refinishing, diesel and heavy equipment mechanics, heavy equipment operator, material handling equipment mechanic.

5. If he is able to do so for next semester, Stone might also consider signing up for a course through his own school or the NESAC Cooperative related to his interest areas. Tim Danson, the coordinator of the cooperative can be contacted at 555-6880 for the NESAC course catalog.

6. If it has not already occurred, participation in a job seeking skills class is also suggested. Stone should concentrate on identifying and capitalizing on his strengths. Other areas of concern include job search techniques, resume writing and job interview skills.

Thank you for this most interesting referral. Should you have any questions regarding the content of this report, please feel free to contact me. All recommendations are based on evaluation results and observations. I look forward to meeting with you to discuss the results of this evaluation.

Sincerely,

Megan Sheridan

Megan Sheridan, M.S.
Vocational Evaluator

APPENDIX E

SOCIAL SECURITY REPORT

The following report was based on a 12 hour (two day) vocational evaluation of an applicant for Social Security disability benefits who was referred by a disability determination examiner. The evaluation, which was conducted by a proprietary (private-for-profit) service, centered on identifying any type of sustained, competitive, vocational capacity the applicant might possess.

Report provided by:

Cincinnati Evaluation Center
Cincinnati, Ohio
Paul S. Meyer, CVE, CWA, Vocational Analyst

CONFIDENTIAL

CINCINNATI EVALUATION CENTER
VOCATIONAL EVALUATION REPORT

NAME: Jane Doe

DOB: January 3, 1956   SSAN: 123-45-6789

REFERRED BY: Ohio Bureau of Disability Determination
Examiner X111

SCHEDULING

Date of contact for scheduling: January 20, 1986

PROGRAM DATES

February 3, 4, 1986; six hours in program each day

DATE OF REPORT

February 7, 1986

ALLEGED IMPAIRMENTS

"Aneurysm of brain; Stroke"

ESTABLISHED MEDICAL IMPAIRMENTS (By Severity)

"WAIS-R, Full Scale IQ 85 (9/6/85); Organic brain syndrome; S/P craniotomy; S/P cerebral thrombosis"

RESTRICTIONS PLACED ON APPLICANT

"State Agency Physician suggests unlimited functional capacity."

STATEMENT OF PROBLEM AND DESIRED RESULTS

"Client is an applicant for Social Security disability benefits. We need to know if this 30 year old female worker has the vocational capacity to adjust to any type of competitive employment on a sustained basis. We also need observations and descriptions of function in order to establish a 'mental RFC'. This should include the worker's ability to understand, remember and carry out instructions as well as the capacity to respond appropriately to supervisors, co-workers and customary work pressures."

Report contains seven pages including this cover page:

Program Results	Page 2	Employment History	Page 4
Observations	Page 4	Work Sampling	Page 6

Text is produced on IBM Displaywriter System Word Processing Equipment

923 Carew Tower, Cincinnati, Ohio 45202

Jane Doe
SSAN: 123-45-6789

PROGRAM RESULTS

Ms. Doe does not appear to possess the vocational capacity to adjust to sustained competitive employment at the present time.

During work samples, she had frequent difficulty using her right hand (although she identified her right hand as her leading hand), and when possible she relied on her left hand. She regularly wore glasses for assignments and there were no indications of any vision difficulties.

Ms. Doe was able to remember instructions for basic one and two step assignments, and was able to complete more complex samples such as Valpar #6 - Independent Problem Solving. However during bookkeeping (Valpar #5), she had difficulty understanding and remembering procedure for switching from adding to subtracting on the adding machine, and needed considerable assistance to do this. She used her right hand for entering numbers in the adding machine keypad and for writing entries on ledger sheets, but had difficulty performing the movements which this entailed. Handwriting of numbers was shaky, but legible. In addition to having problems picking up a pencil and writing, she also had difficulty with turning movements required to manipulate screwdrivers with her right hand during Valpar #1 - Small Tools Mechanical.

Ms. Doe did not demonstrate any significant coordination, hand tool use, or assembly ability. A bimanual assembly task (Valpar #8), usually performed from standing, was discontinued because of leg pain she reported, which she said is related to blood clotting she has experienced in her legs. She worked for approximately half the normally assigned time and completed a low number of assemblies, which likely reflects her coordination limitations.

Ms. Doe did achieve good scores for accuracy on a size discrimination assignment selecting proper sized nuts to fit on a variety of bolts (Valpar #2), alphabetical filing (Valpar #5), problem solving (Valpar #6), and sorting (Valpar #7), but speed was slow on these assignments, which seemed a function of coordination limitations and problems with right hand grasp and use. Her best performance was on mail sorting (Valpar #5), but speed was still slow, and no overall sample results were at the level considered consistent with entry employability (see Work Sampling).

Therefore, in summary, Ms. Doe does not appear to possess the vocational capacity to adjust to sustained competitive employment at this time, even though she was able to maintain concentration, and to understand, remember, and apply most task instructions (it is noted, however, that Ms. Doe did get lost returning from the washroom and needed help in finding the Center's offices; otherwise her brother brought her and accompanied her to lunch). While she was able to

Jane Doe
SSAN: 123-45-6789

complete five assignments effectively in terms of accuracy, speed was slow, which in most instances appeared related to coordination problems and hand use limitations.

Additionally, physical tolerance appeared limited, especially for standing tasks, and Ms. Doe reported leg pain indicating that she has had blood clots there and that her legs swell. She seemed to become more fatigued during tasks requiring motor abilities and coordination than she did on tasks that required primarily verbal skills. She looked very tired by the close of the program. Because she appeared to become easily fatigued, other samples were not administered.

While referral material indicates Ms. Doe has had speech difficulties in the past and throat spasms, her speech was clearly understandable, without pressure, and was managed by her during the program without apparent difficulty. She established good relations with members of the staff, and appeared able to manage the stress of the program. There were no observed changes in mood, she applied herself fully to assignments, and seemed to have exceptional frustration tolerance. Ms. Doe was highly cooperative.

Paul S. Meyer, Vocational Analyst
Certified Vocational Evaluator No. 1
Certified Work Adjustment Specialist No. 1

Jane Doe
SSAN: 123-45-6789

PROGRAM OBSERVATIONS

Ms. Doe was brought by her brother. She wore slacks and blouses, and seemed very careful about personal appearance. She looked her stated height and weight of 5' 4", 145 lbs. She regularly wore glasses.

The afternoon of the first day Ms. Doe got lost returning from the washroom. She said she ended up on the first floor of the Center's office building and a guard assisted her in coming back to the Center. She commented that she gets lost at times when driving near where she lives, if she attempts to get to a destination by way of a different route than that which she regularly uses.

Ms. Doe seemed to become more fatigued during tasks requiring motor abilities and coordination than she did on tasks that required primarily verbal skills. She seemed to have particular difficulty using her right hand for grasping and picking up items. She also reported leg pain when standing even for short periods of time. She looked very tired by the close of the program, with darkened circles under her eyes.

[Weather, Monday, February 3, Tuesday, February 4, 1986: Cloudy skies with morning temperatures in the low twenties; air quality 37 and 29 respectively, good and better than clean air standards.]

BACKGROUND AND EMPLOYMENT HISTORY

Ms. Doe said she was born January 3, 1956, in Dayton, Ohio, and graduated from high school there in 1974. She said she then went to work at a company that made candles, and operated a machine that cut candles to length doing this for a year and a half.

She married and moved with her husband, who was in the Marines, to North Carolina. She said she had a daughter and stayed at home to take care of her. They moved to Illinois for several years and Ms. Doe continued to stay at home caring for her daughter.

They then moved to the Cincinnati area and she worked at a company manufacturing appliance switches. She said she worked on the assembly line putting switch parts together for a while, but mostly did packing and was there five years.

She said she kept getting laid off from this job, so she went to school to become a Licensed Practical Nurse. She said she started having bad headaches during the third semester and couldn't concentrate. She said one day something felt like an explosion in her head, which was later discovered to be an aneurysm, and then five and a half weeks after this, in January, 1985, she had a stroke while she was a patient

Jane Doe
SSAN: 123-45-6789

in a Cincinnati hospital for tests. In February, 1985, she went to the hospital again because of blood clotting. She said she sees her physician once a month and takes Bentyl for throat spasms, aspirin to prevent blood clotting, and Lasix. She described various exercises that she does at home to strengthen her hands but is not currently under any therapy program.

Other health history includes her saying she was in an auto accident in 1977, and suffered a broken rib, internal bleeding, bruised arms, and glass cuts on her face and throat. She said she has no residuals from this now. She also reports having gall bladder surgery.

Ms. Doe said she is divorced, and lives in an apartment with her 10 year old daughter. She said she receives ADC at $30.00 per week and food stamps at $107.00 per month. She said she is supposed to get some child support but doesn't receive it. She said she has a current Ohio driver's license and drives a 1970 Chevrolet, but has no special assists on the car and only drives close to home. She said she takes walks and does hand exercises, and cleans and takes care of her apartment. Ms. Doe said she reads but if she tries to do this for very long she has trouble with her eyes, however she said this condition has been improving. She reports having no military service.

WORK SAMPLING

NAME: Jane Doe
DOB: January 3, 1956   SSAN: 123-45-6789
ADMINISTERED: February 3, 4, 1986

Scores are based on MTM (Methods-Time-Measurement) standards from Valpar Corporation. 100 percent for both speed and accuracy indicates performance comparable to entry level employability. Relationship to occupations is in Dictionary of Occupational Titles worker traits codes.

VALPAR #1 - SMALL TOOLS MECHANICAL (Panel #1 - Speed 25%) hand tool use in a confined space; occupations dealing with things code .881: Ms. Doe was assigned the first panel of the task involving installation of screws using screwdrivers. She worked from sitting and wore her glasses. She used her left hand to start the screws and both hands to turn the screwdrivers. When she attempted using her right hand alone to do this, she had little control over the screwdriver and made a pushing-type motion at the screws, rather than a turning motion. Because of her apparent difficulty manipulating the screwdrivers, no further panels were assigned.

VALPAR #2 - SIZE DISCRIMINATION (Speed 5% Accuracy 150%) selecting nuts to fit a variety of bolts; things .884: Worked from standing and wore her glasses. She chose to use her left non-dominant hand for the task, saying she has been using her left hand a lot since her stroke, and that it was easier for her on a task of this type. She made no errors but speed was slow.

VALPAR #5 - CLERICAL COMPREHENSION AND APTITUDE (Alphabetical Filing Speed 60% Accuracy 135%; Mail Sorting Speed 70% Accuracy 150%; Bookkeeping Speed 5% Accuracy 5%;) ability to perform basic clerical tasks; data .388: Ms. Doe completed clerical tasks from sitting and wore her glasses. During alphabetical filing she needed two short breaks, reporting she had a persistent "tickle" in her throat. She said she has had this problem since her stroke. She had difficulty picking up file cards, especially with her right hand. She made two errors. She used her left non-dominant hand exclusively for mail sorting, and made no errors. She performed all three sections of bookkeeping, but had difficulty completing the daily log which involves frequent switching from adding to subtracting on the adding machine. The change in process appeared to confuse her and she needed much assistance during this section. It was also noted she had difficulty picking up a pencil from the table with her right hand and used only the middle finger on her right hand to enter numbers in the keypad of the adding machine. Handwriting of numbers on ledger sheets was shaky, but legible. She made a total of eleven errors on bookkeeping and speed was slow.

VALPAR #6 - INDEPENDENT PROBLEM SOLVING (Speed 70% Accuracy 135%) matching geometric designs by color and shape; data .388: Ms. Doe worked from sitting, wore her glasses, used her right hand to mark her responses on the answer sheet, and her left hand to turn pages in the test booklet. She understood instructions without problem and made only two errors. Speed was slow.

Jane Doe
SSAN: 123-45-6789

VALPAR #7 - MULTI-LEVEL SORTING (Speed 55% Accuracy 100%) sorting chips by color, letter, number and combinations; data .288, .388: Ms. Doe worked from sitting, wore her glasses and alternated hands to distribute chips. She had some difficulty grasping chips with the fingers of her right hand. She made one error.

VALPAR #8 - SIMULATED ASSEMBLY simulates conveyor-assembly jobs; performed from standing for twenty minutes .886 and .887: Worked from standing, wore her glasses and used both hands to make assemblies. She worked for five minutes, and then seemed fatigued, so a break was taken. She returned to the task in the afternoon, but at five minutes seventeen seconds said her left leg was bothering her because of blood clotting she had there in the past, so the sample was discontinued by the administrator, and accordingly no scores are reportable. She had completed 86 correct assemblies in the time she had worked on the task, a low number which appears to reflect her coordination and hand grasp limitations.

VALPAR #11 - EYE-HAND-FOOT COORDINATION (Speed 60% Accuracy 45%) three trials from sitting, each consists of maneuvering nine steel balls through a maze using hand and foot controls; machine or equipment operation .882: Ms. Doe wore her glasses. She used both hands on the hand controls and both feet on the treadle. She was able to acquire a higher number of points with each trial, but scores for both speed and accuracy were low.

Paul S. Meyer, Vocational Analyst
Certified Vocational Evaluator No. 1
Certified Work Adjustment Specialist No. 1

APPENDIX F

WORKER'S COMPENSATION REPORT

This report is based on a two full day vocational evaluation of an injured worker referred by his employer (a self-insured company). Since he was unable to return to his previous job after a work related injury, the evaluation attempted to identify other direct employment options.

Report provided by:

Ellis and Associates, Incorporated
Chicago, Illinois
Debra Homa, CRC, Rehabilitation Specialist
Steven M. Blumenthal, M.S., CRC, CVE, Rehabilitation Supervisor
Cindy R. Ellis, CRC, CVE, President

Ellis and Associates, Inc.

300 W. Grand, Suite 500
Chicago, Illinois 60610
(312) 645-1214

NAME: Robert Johnson

ADDRESS: 1845 Lake St.
Forest Park, IL 60130

PHONE: 312/366-4785
AGE: 32

REFERRED BY: Mary Blakely
General Companies, Inc.
SOCIAL SECURITY NUMBER: 356-47-1543
EMPLOYER: General Food Stores
EVALUATION DATES: 2/11-12/86

BACKGROUND INFORMATION

The client is a 32-year-old, married, Caucasian male who reports a workers' compensation injury to his lower back which occurred on 3/25/85 while working as a night grocery clerk for General Food Stores. The client's medical treatment is described in-depth in progress reports from our rehabilitation nurse and will only be briefly summarized. Previous reports indicate that Mr. Johnson was diagnosed as having a bulging disc at the L4-5 levels. He completed the River Forest Pain Treatment Center on 1/10/86 with restrictions as follows: he can sit for an 8-hour day; he can stand for two hours and walk for three hours; he should not do repetitive bending, twisting or lifting; he should do no crawling or climbing; he can lift infrequently from 35 to 50 lbs. but should not lift more than 50 lbs.

Mr. Johnson's treating physician is Dr. Mark Bensen, orthopedic surgeon. The client states that Dr. Bensen has told him that there is a "95 percent chance" that he will eventually need back surgery. However, recent medical reports from Dr. Ronald Peters and from Dr. Gary Graham indicate that they did not believe the client should have surgery.

VOCATIONAL BACKGROUND

At the time of his injury, Mr. Johnson was employed as a night grocery clerk at General Food Stores; he had held this job about six months before his accident. He explains that his duties included stocking shelves and bringing loads into the store, and that the job required constant lifting, bending, and stooping. He previously worked for about five years as a machine operator at Payne Corporation, a division of General; he had to leave this job when this division closed.

The client is a high school graduate. He reports that in 1981 and 1982, he attended Triton College on a part-time basis; he states that he took courses in industrial engineering and management. He explains that he stopped attending school after his employer discontinued its tuition reimbursement program, as he felt he could not afford to pay for school.

The client reports that he has about 15 years of experience in construction (he says that he began this work when he was very young) and that he has also been a construction crew supervisor in the past. He relates that he is familiar with various aspects of construction, such as concrete, drywall, and carpentry.

VOCATIONAL APPRAISAL
(Refer to Appendix for description of tests and work samples)

Achievement Profile

Wide Range Achievement Test (WRAT), Level II

Arithmetic: Above 12th grade

Micro Computer Evaluation and Screening Instrument - MESA

Academic Skills

Mathematics:	5th grade level
Vocabulary:	10th grade level
Reading:	12th grade level
Spelling:	Greater than 10th grade level

Arithmetic skills included the ability to add, subtract, multiply, divide, and perform calculations involving fractions, decimals, percentages, and units of measurement. He could also solve basic algebra problems. Results of academic testing also indicated reading and spelling skills to be roughly commensurate with his level of education. Thus, he should be able to read involved instructions and technical reports, as well as to communicate in writing. It was believed that his mathematics score on the MESA was not an accurate assessment of his math skills; it was possible that he selected his answers too quickly when doing this test, rather than working some of them out on scratch paper.

Aptitude Profile

Raven's Standard Progressive Matrices
    Compared to other individuals of age group:
                                    95th percentile

Bennett Mechanical Comprehension Test
    Compared to industrial applicants for union
    apprenticeships in the construction trade: 40th
                                    percentile

Revised Minnesota Paper Form Board Test
    Compared to male applicants for assembly jobs:
                                    75th percentile

SRA Verbal Form
    Compared to Educational Norms
    Language Score: 80th percentile
    Quantitative Score: 98th percentile

    Total Score compared to computer programmers: 93rd
                                    percentile

Personnel Tests for Industry/Oral Directions Test
Compared to machine operators: 90th percentile

Minnesota Clerical Test
    Compared to male clerks
    Name Comparison: 85th percentile
    Number Comparison: 97th percentile

How Supervise?
    Compared to operating supervisors: 45th percentile
    Compared to top management: 10th percentile

MESA Sub-tests

Vision screening:	95th percentile
Size discrimination:	95th percentile
Color discrimination:	High
Problem solving:	High Average
Visual memory:	High

Results of aptitude testing indicate above average to superior ability in numerous areas. His test performance suggested excellent non-verbal abstract reasoning ability, which should enable him to learn and apply abstract concepts and to use logical thinking to solve complex problems. It should be noted that he completed this test in about 15 minutes, while most individuals take about 45 minutes to finish this test.

Results of aptitude testing also indicate excellent numerical reasoning ability, suggesting that he could work quickly and easily with numbers, such as to compute costs and perform accounting. He also showed above average verbal reasoning which would be important in jobs requiring oral and written communication. In addition, results indicated excellent ability to quickly and accurately perceive letters and numbers (clerical perception).

Results also indicated above average spatial perception (the ability to mentally visualize two and three-dimensional forms in space); this ability would be important in a variety of tasks, such as reading blueprints.

He demonstrated only average understanding of management principles and supervisory practices; in view of his previous classes in management, it was expected that he would have obtained a higher score in this area. Test results suggested average understanding of basic mechanical principles and physical laws.

<u>Dexterity Profile</u>

MESA Sub-tests

Eye-hand coordination:	60th percentile
Eye-hand-foot coordination:	90th percentile
Fine Finger-Dominant:	85th percentile
Fine Finger-Non-Dominant:	95th percentile

Wiring: 85th percentile

Results of dexterity testing indicate above average finger dexterity, eye-hand coordination, and eye-hand-foot coordination skills.

Work Sample Assessment

VALPAR Clerical Comprehension and Aptitude Work Sample

Bookkeeping section only:
Work Speed: 145 percent   MTM
Work Accuracy: 100 percent MTM

VALPAR Independent Problem Solving Work Sample

Speed: 120 percent MTM
Accuracy: 150 percent MTM
Compared to employed workers: 80th   percentile

VALPAR Tri-Level Measurement Work Sample

Speed: 110 percent MTM
Accuracy: Greater than 150 percent MTM
Compared to individuals in a skills training center:
                                    96th percentile

Situtational Assessment

VALPAR Money Handling

He showed satisfactory knowledge of information pertaining to banking and and credit, but his performance suggested limited knowledge of economics related to business; in particular, he showed very limited understanding of insurance and taxes, and he had difficulty calculating interest and credit.

VALPAR Drafting

He was given two sections of this work sample which required him to measure and to read blueprints. His performance indicated good measuring skills, but he needed some review in measuring in centimeters. He also demonstrated basic blueprint reading skills, although he did not seem to be familiar with certain blueprint terminology, such as "extension lines" and "object lines."

Results of work sample testing indicate that the client shows above average potential in the following areas: numerical record-keeping, quality control/inspection, and the ability to pay attention to important detail and to find and record errors.

Vocational Exploration

Career Occupational Preference System

Results of this interest inventory indicate high interest in professional business, with above average interest in clerical, professional arts, and communication. Below average interest was found in the areas of professional science, outdoor, skilled arts, and skilled service.

Examples of jobs which corresponded with his interest profile include: accountant, manager, teller, accounting clerk, architect, and technical writer.

MESA Vocational Interest Areas

His responses indicated a preference for the following general interest areas: a preference for work dealing with things and objects; a liking for work that involves business contact with people; and a special liking for work of an abstract and creative nature.

Mr. Johnson said that he enjoyed working with numbers; he explained that he had been interested in industrial engineering because he liked to devise more efficient ways of doing things and to cut costs.

FUNCTIONAL VOCATIONAL TOLERANCES

VALPAR Simulated Assembly

Number of correct assemblies: 95 percent MTM

This work sample required him to work from a standing position for approximately 25 minutes and to work with both hands simultaneously. Upon completion of this task, he complained of soreness in his lower back. Nevertheless, it did not appear that this reported discomfort significantly interfered with his performance, since his production rate for this task was at a competitive level (100% MTM represents competitive-level proficiency). Throughout the consecutive two-day evaluation, Mr. Johnson was observed working from a seated position for prolonged periods of time. He reported feeling increased soreness in his lower back on the second day of evaluation, but this did not noticeably affect his performance.

WORK BEHAVIORS/TEMPERAMENT

Mr. Johnson was very cooperative and friendly throughout the evaluation. He related that he was aware that opportunities for alternate employment at General may be limited, and he indicated that he was receptive to job placement outside this organization. In fact, he expressed strong motivation to resume working in some capacity, as he stated that his injury had occurred almost one year ago and that he was ready to get on with his life. Initially, he indicated that he was interested in being given extensive training, such as completing a bachelors degree; it was explained to him that such training generally was not required within the workers' compensation system, and he verbalized acceptance of these limitations.

SUMMARY

The client is a 32-year-old, married, Caucasian male who reports a workers' compensation injury to his lower back which occurred on 3/25/85 while working as a night grocery clerk for General Food Stores. Previous reports indicate that Mr. Johnson was diagnosed as having a bulging disc at the L4-5 levels. He completed the River Forest Pain Treatment Center on 1/10/86 with restrictions as follows: he can sit for an 8-hour day; he can stand for two hours and walk for three hours; he should not do repetitive bending, twisting or lifting; he should do no crawling or climbing; he can lift infrequently from 35 to 50 lbs. but should not lift more than 50 lbs.

The client is a high school graduate. He reports that in 1981 and 1982, he attended Triton College and took courses in industrial engineering and management. The client reports that he has about 15 years of experience in construction and that he has also been a construction crew supervisor in the past. He relates that he is familiar with various aspects of construction, such as concrete, drywall, and carpentry.

Overall evaluation testing indicates the following assets and liabilities:

Assets

1. Superior non-verbal abstract reasoning ability.
2. Excellent numerical reasoning, above average verbal reasoning.
3. Above average finger dexterity and coordination.
4. Above average spatial and clerical perception.
5. Ability to follow verbal instructions.
6. Academic skills.
7. Average mechanical comprehension.
8. Ability to perform numerical record-keeping.
9. Ability to perform inspection/quality control.
10. Basic knowledge of blueprint reading.

Liabilities

1. Limited knowledge of economics related to business.
2. Physical restrictions.

Results of testing suggest aptitude, interests, and physical capacities to be compatible with the occupations listed below. These are considered representative but not all inclusive of the client's vocational options.

DOT Code	Job Title
160.267-018	Estimator
187.167-142	Manager, Service Dept.
183.167-018	General Supervisor
182.167-026	Superintendent, Construction
185.167-046	Manager, Retail Store

221.167-018   Production Coordinator
162.157-038   Purchasing Agent
162.157-022   Assistant Buyer

RECOMMENDATIONS

1. We will discuss the evaluation results during a meeting with General representatives on 2/20/86.

2. If placement within General is not feasible, it is recommended that the client receive job placement assistance.

If you have any questions with this report or recommendations as outlined above, please let me know.

Sincerely,

Ellis and Associates

BY: _____
Debra Homa, C.R.C.
Rehabilitation Specialist

BY: _____
Steven M. Blumenthal, M.S., C.R.C., C.V.E.
Rehabilitation Supervisor

Enclosure: Appendix

APPENDIX

Aptitude Tests

Raven's Standard Progressive Matrices Test
Assesses non-verbal abstract reasoning ability and requires attention to visual detail and pattern recognition.

Bennett Mechanical Comprehension Test
Is designed to measure the individual's knowledge of physical laws and mechanical principles, an important aptitude for jobs involving the repair and/or operation of complex mechanical devices.

Revised Minnesota Paper Form Board Test
Assesses spatial aptitude, the ability to mentally visualize three-dimensional objects from two-dimensional drawings.

College Qualifications Tests
These are a series of three ability tests developed to be broadly predictive of college success.

General Clerical Test
This test measures a variety of clerical aptitudes, such as proofreading, filing, basic business math, spelling, vocabulary, and reading comprehension. Emphasis is placed on both speed and accuracy.

Computer Operator Aptitude Test Battery
Assesses ability to perform sequence recognition, format checking, and logical thinking, which are traits necessary for successful completion of both training and employment in the field of computer operations.

Computer Programmer Aptitude Test Battery
Measures aptitudes in the areas of verbal ability, reasoning, number ability, diagramming, and perceiving letter series, traits needed to successfully complete training and employment in computer programming.

Personnel Classification Test
This test assesses numerical and verbal ability in comparison to a variety of industrial and educational norm groups.

Minnesota Clerical Test
Assesses the individual's ability to quickly and accurately compare pairs of numbers and names in comparison to various clerical workers.

Oral Directions Test
Measures ability to follow oral directions in completing written information. General mental ability is required in analyzing oral directions which increase in complexity; also requires ability to concentrate.

SRA Verbal Test
This is a basic mental ability test which assesses verbal and numerical reasoning skills.

How Supervise?
Assesses knowledge and insight regarding human relations and supervisory

practices which promote worker productivity.

Dexterity Tests

Purdue Pegboard Test
Involves using the right, left, and both hands to perform fine finger dexterity operations without the use of tools.

Crawford Small Parts Dexterity Test
Assesses fine finger dexterity and eye-hand coordination using tweezers and a screwdriver.

Minnesota Rate of Manipulation Test
Assesses ability to work with the hands, wrists, and arms in placing and turning two-inch blocks.

VALPAR Size Discrimination Work Sample
Assesses gross manual dexterity, visual size discrimination, and bilateral coordination in the assembly and dissassembly of various sized nuts onto threaded bolts.

Interest Tests

Career Occupational Preference System
This interest inventory identifies occupational preferences in 14 vocational clusters, ranging from unskilled through skilled and technical/professional positions.

Wide Range Interest and Opinion Test
This is a non-verbal, pictorial interest inventory.

Strong Campbell Interest Inventory
Assesses general occupational interests as well as specific job preferences and is geared toward professional occupations.

Career Assessment Inventory
Assesses general occupational interests as well as specific job preferences and is geared toward semi-technical occupations.

Minnesota Importance Questionnaire
Assesses work needs as they relate to perceived job satisfaction.

Achievement Tests
The following are used to measure the individual's ability to solve numerical and verbal problems, including general math, algebra, spelling, vocabulary, reading, editing, etc.

Gates-MacGinitie Reading Test
Wide Range Achievement Test
SRA Reading Index
SRA Arithmetic Index
Peabody Individual Achievement Test

VALPAR Work Samples

Small Tools (Mechanical)
Measures the individual's knowledge of small hand tools; also assesses manual dexterity and physical tolerance.

Numerical Sorting
Measures ability to sort, file, and categorize objects by alpha/numeric code.

Clerical Comprehension and Aptitude
Measures a person's ability to perform a variety of clerical tasks, such as telephone answering, alphabetical filing, mail sorting, and bookkeeping.

Independent Problem Solving
Assesses ability to perform work tasks which require a visual comparison of colors and shapes. Decision-making and instruction following are emphasized. Ability to pay attention to detail and adapt to a specific routine are also addressed.

Simulated Assembly
Measures ability to work at assembly tasks requiring repetitious, physical manipulation and bi-lateral use of upper extremities.

Whole Body Range of Motion
Non-medical measure of gross body movement of the trunk, arms, hands, legs, and fingers, as they relate to physical capacities to perform job tasks.

Tri-Level Measurement
Measures ability to perform very simple to very precise inspection and measurement tasks. Also assesses ability to follow set techniques or procedures and to exercise judgment and decision-making skills.

Eye-Hand-Foot Coordination
Measures ability to use eyes, hands, and feet simultaneously and in a coordinated manner.

Soldering and Inspection
Measures ability to learn and apply basic skills necessary to perform soldering tasks at varying levels of difficulty.

Money Handling
Measures skills in dealing with monetary concepts, ranging from basic money recognition to consumer economics.

Electrical Circuitry and Print Reading
Measures ability to understand and apply principles and functions of electrical circuits, ranging from simple circuit testing to construction of circuits utilizing schematics.

Drafting
Measures potential to compete in an entry-level position requiring basic drafting skills, such as simple measuring, line perception, determining scale dimensions, drawing diagrams, free-hand drawing, and interpreting blueprints.

APPENDIX G

APTICOM REPORT

The following system dedicated report is only one of a variety of APTICOM report formats ranging in length from two to over thirty pages (the length of this report is eighteen pages). A longer report was used to give an example of the different categories and options available for inclusion in an APTICOM report. However, selected pages that provide legends (descriptions of various terms) have been removed to reduce the overall length of the report. The format allows for the addition of comments if needed. The report is based on a one and-one-half hour assessment conducted in a special services unit within the school district, on a tenth grade special needs student referred by his high school. The resulting document was used for purposes of counseling and placement in a vocational technical secondary school.

Report provided by:

Vocational Research Institute
Philadelphia, Pennsylvania
Howard Dansky, Senior Research Associate
Randy Lindsey, Director of Product Development

APTICOM A5   PAGE 1

NAME: JACK STAGG   ID#: 007   DATE: 6/5/86
FACILITY: VOCATIONAL RESEARCH INSTITUTE

REMARKS:
  THIS REPORT USES 10TH GRADE SCORING STANDARDS AND APTITUDE SCORE ADJUSTMENT
FOR STANDARD ERRORS OF MEASURE.

REPORT OPTIONS SELECTED

BATTERIES INCLUDED:

    APTITUDE TEST BATTERY
    OCCUPATIONAL INTEREST INVENTORY
    EDUCATIONAL SKILLS DEVELOPMENT BATTERY

REPORT FORMAT:
    COMPREHENSIVE SCORE REPORT

VOCATIONAL RECOMMENDATIONS:
    WORK GROUPS WITH NARRATIVE AND JOB TITLES

LEGEND:
    APTITUDE CODES
    INTEREST AREAS
    GENERAL EDUCATION DEVELOPMENT
    SPECIFIC VOCATIONAL PREPARATION

DATA BASE:
    APTITUDE TEST BATTERY, 10 th GRADE WITH SEM
    OCCUPATIONAL INTEREST INVENTORY, PREVOCATIONAL

REPORTS INCLUDED

APTITUDE TEST BATTERY, COMPREHENSIVE SCORE REPORT
OCCUPATIONAL INTEREST INVENTORY, COMPREHENSIVE SCORE REPORT
EDUCATIONAL SKILLS DEVELOPMENT BATTERY, COMPREHENSIVE SCORE REPORT
VOCATIONAL RECOMMENDATIONS:
    WORK GROUPS WITH NARRATIVE AND JOB TITLES

APTICOM A5   PAGE   2

NAME: JACK STAGG   ID#: 007   DATE: 6/5/86

                    APTITUDE TEST BATTERY
                    COMPREHENSIVE SCORE REPORT

SECTION I.   SUBTEST SCORES

The table below presents subtest raw scores, number of items attempted, and standard scores which correspond to raw scores. Raw scores report the number of correct answers on perceptual and cognitive tests or the number of cycles completed in the motor coordination or dexterity tests. Standard scores show how your raw scores compare to scores achieved by a group of adults who were given these tests. A standard score of 100 is exactly average. Scores from 80 to 120 can be thought of as "in the average range."

SUBTEST	RAW SCORES	NUMBER OF ATTEMPTS	STANDARD SCORES
1 Object Identification	22	22	126
2 Abstract Shape Matching	19	25	105
3 Clerical Matching	14	18	107
4 Eye-Hand-Foot Coordination	44	44	97
5 Pattern Visualization	11	18	80
6 Computation	12	16	98
7 Finger Dexterity	23	23	107
8 Numerical Reasoning	10	16	84
9 Manual Dexterity	49	49	115
10 Word Meanings	16	16	86
11 Eye-Hand Coordination	73	73	111

APTICOM A5   PAGE 3

NAME: JACK STAGG   ID#: 007   DATE: 6/5/86

APTITUDE TEST BATTERY
COMPREHENSIVE SCORE REPORT

SECTION II.   INDIVIDUAL APTITUDE PROFILE

      The profile reports and graphically presents your aptitudes as standard scores and as percentile scores. Both types of scores involve the comparison of your performance against the performance of 10th graders.

      The aptitude codes, listed in the column on the far left, are defined in the legend at the end of the last report. Different groups of aptitudes are important in different jobs. Aptitude scores are created by combining and/or recomputing subtest scores. An aptitude score of 100 is exactly average. Scores from 80 to 120 can be thought of as " in the average range. " The graph of your aptitude scores displays your relative strengths. Differences between these scores are important in career planning. Percentile scores report the percentage of people who score below you. (Adjusted scores, reported in the far right column, can be explained to you by your counselor.)

```
                                                        (ADJUSTED)
   CODE       SCORE     BAV     AVG     AAV   % STANDING  (SCORE)
     G          93     . ..... ...X..... ..... .     36        99
     V          92     . ..... ...X..... ..... .     35        97
     N         101     . ..... ....X.... ..... .     52       106
     S          85     . ..... .X....... ..... .     23        91
     P         116     . ..... ........X  ..... .    79       121
     Q         112     . ..... .......X.  ..... .    73       122
     K         116     . ..... ........X  ..... .    79       126
     F         111     . ..... .......X.  ..... .    71       119
     M         117     . ..... ........X  ..... .    80       125
     E          97     . ..... ....X.... ..... .     44       108
```

APTICOM A5   PAGE 4

NAME: JACK STAGG   ID#: 007   DATE: 6/5/86

OCCUPATIONAL INTEREST INVENTORY
COMPREHENSIVE SCORE REPORT

The U. S. Department of Labor divides all jobs into twelve groupings (Interest Areas) based on the kinds of activities workers do in each one (see legend for complete descriptions). This report shows how closely your interests match these activities to help you choose the kind of work you will most enjoy.

SECTION I. INTEREST AREA SCORES AND PERCENTILES

Your total number of "LIKE", "?", and "DISLIKE" answers for each Interest Area appears below. Percentile scores show the percentage of other people who gave fewer "LIKE" answers than you did in each area. A percentile score of 50 shows average interest; 70 or higher shows above average interest. Under M / F are percentiles comparing your answers to males (M) and females (F) separately. Under M / F you should focus on the percentile for your own sex.

INTEREST AREA	LIKE	?	DISLIKE	PERCENTILE (TOTAL)	PERCENTILE (M / F)
01 ARTISTIC	4	4	7	53	59/46
02 SCIENTIFIC	6	2	6	81	84/74
03 PLANTS/ANIMALS	3	2	8	64	64/63
04 PROTECTIVE	11	1	1	93	91/96
05 MECHANICAL	6	2	6	81	68/93
06 INDUSTRIAL	0	3	10	28	28/23
07 BUSINESS DETAIL	0	2	14	15	24/ 7
08 SELLING	0	3	7	18	23/13
09 ACCOMMODATING	1	0	9	33	42/24
10 HUMANITARIAN	4	1	9	59	76/45
11 LEAD/INFLUENCE	5	2	9	61	68/52
12 PHYS. PERFORMING	5	1	8	61	45/78

APTICOM A5   PAGE 5

NAME: JACK STAGG   ID#: 007   DATE: 6/5/86

OCCUPATIONAL INTEREST INVENTORY
COMPREHENSIVE SCORE REPORT

SECTION II. INDIVIDUAL INTEREST PROFILE

The profile below lets you see and compare your standard scores for the twelve Interest Areas. Like percentile scores, standard scores are based on a comparison of your totals of "LIKE" answers to other people's totals. An average standard score is anywhere from 91 to 110. An "X" under AVERAGE means you show about the same amount of interest in that Interest Area as most people. An "X" under High means that you show more than average interest in that area.

INTEREST AREA	SS	LOW	AVERAGE	HIGH
01 ARTISTIC	97	....	. X . . .	....
02 SCIENTIFIC	117	....	. . . . .	.X............
03 PLANTS/ANIMALS	102	....	. . X . .	....
04 PROTECTIVE	136	....	. . . . .	......X.......
05 MECHANICAL	117	....	. . . . .	.X............
06 INDUSTRIAL	88	X	. . . . .	....
07 BUSINESS DETAIL	81	..........X..	. . . . .	....
08 SELLING	83	...........X.	. . . . .	....
09 ACCOMMODATING	86	...........X.	. . . . .	....
10 HUMANITARIAN	98	....	. X . . .	....
11 LEAD/INFLUENCE	101	....	. . X . .	....
12 PHYS. PERFORMING	104	....	. . . X .	....

SECTION III. INDIVIDUAL PROFILE ANALYSIS (IPA)

The IPA makes a comparison among your totals of LIKE answers for all twelve Interest Areas. The interest areas listed below are the ones that stand out above your own average level of interest.

HIGH INTEREST AREAS
02 SCIENTIFIC
04 PROTECTIVE
05 MECHANICAL

Look over your percentile scores, Standard Scores, and IPA. Explore your most consistently high Interest Areas further by reading in the Guide for Occupational Exploration (GOE) (U.S. Department of Labor, 1979). Work with your counselor to find job choices which combine your interests as much as possible and which match your abilities.

APTICOM A5   PAGE 6

NAME: JACK STAGG   ID#: 007   DATE: 6/5/86

              EDUCATIONAL SKILLS DEVELOPMENT BATTERY
                   COMPREHENSIVE SCORE REPORT

SECTION I. SCALE SCORES

     The table below reports the number of correct responses, the
number of items attempted and the highest possible score for each
scale within the mathematics and language tests. When an "X" is
reported in the far right column, under " Cut-Off Achieved ", the
"X" indicates that there is evidence that you have mastered skills
at the identified level(s).

Educational Development Level	Number Correct	Number Attempted	Maximum Score	Cut-off Achieved
Language 1	7	7	7	X
Language 2	5	7	7	X
Language 3	4	8	8	
Language 4	1	8	8	
Math 1	6	7	7	X
Math 2	0	7	7	
Math 3	0	1	8	
Math 4	0	0	8	

APTICOM A5   PAGE   7

NAME: JACK STAGG   ID#: 007   DATE: 6/5/86

SECTION II. PERFORMANCE ANALYSIS

     The table below reports an analysis of your results by topic
area. The number reported to the left of a slash is the number of
correct responses; the number to the right of a slash is the number
of items of that type on the test. A review of these findings may
help you identify your areas of greatest strength or weakness.

A. LANGUAGE DEVELOPMENT

Topic Area	Scale 1	Scale 2	Scale 3	Scale 4	Totals
Spell/Vocab	2/ 2			0/ 1	2/ 3
Vocabulary	2/ 2	3/ 3	4/ 5	1/ 4	10/14
Ref Skills	1/ 1	1/ 1	0/ 1	0/ 1	2/ 4
Punct/Caps	1/ 1	1/ 1	0/ 1		2/ 3
Verb Forms	1/ 1	0/ 2	0/ 1	0/ 2	1/ 6
Totals.......	7/ 7	5/ 7	4/ 8	1/ 8	17/30

B. MATHEMATICS DEVELOPMENT

Topic Area	Scale 1	Scale 2	Scale 3	Scale 4	Totals
Computation	5/ 6	0/ 4	0/ 2		5/12
Measurement	1/ 1	0/ 1			1/ 2
Ratio/Percent		0/ 2	0/ 3		0/ 5
Algebra			0/ 1	0/ 2	0/ 3
Geometry			0/ 2	0/ 2	0/ 4
Trigonometry				0/ 4	0/ 4
Totals.......	6/ 7	0/ 7	0/ 8	0/ 8	6/30

APTICOM A5   PAGE 8

NAME: JACK STAGG   ID#: 007   DATE: 6/5/86

                     VOCATIONAL RECOMMENDATIONS

     The U.S. Department of Labor has divided jobs into sixty-six
OAP's (Occupational Aptitude Patterns) based upon similarity of
aptitude score requirements. The sixty-six OAP's are closely
related to the Work Groups which are described in the Guide for
Occupational Exploration (U. S. Department of Labor, 1979).

     Each of the Work Groups listed below falls within your
strongest Interest Areas, as assessed by the APTICOM Occupational
Interest Inventory. These Interest Area titles are reported above
the associated Work Groups for which you have qualified on the
basis of your aptitude scores.

     For each Work Group title listed below you will find the
associated OAP number, with required critical aptitude scores,
as well as the Work Group number (GOE XX.XX).

     Listed beneath the general Work Group information are some
representative job titles from the Work Group. The job titles which
are listed demand math and language development at or below the GED
levels which you achieved on the APTICOM Educational Skills
Development Battery.

     Listed to the right of each job title is the corresponding
DOT (Dictionary of Occupational Titles) occupational code number,
the General Educational Development (GED) requirements for math and
language and a rating for the length of Specific Vocational
Preparation (SVP) that is typically required. Your counselor will
be able to tell you how to find a DOT number/job title and its
corresponding job description in the Dictionary of Occupational
Titles. GED and SVP rating definitions are reported in legends at
the end of the Vocational Recommendations Report.

     Your performance on the APTICOM Educational Skills Development
Battery suggests that you may wish to explore specific occupations
within the Work Groups which demand the following math and language
skill development levels:
                         Math   Language
                          1   2
                                       1

APTICOM A5   PAGE 9

INTEREST AREA 05 MECHANICAL

OAP 23   S 085   P 080   M 085
GOE 05.08   LAND & MOTOR VEHICLE OPERATION

Workers in this group drive large or small trucks, delivery vans,
or locomotives, to move materials or deliver products. Some drive
ambulances; others operate small boats.

    Refer to pages 108 to 109 in the Guide for Occupational
    Exploration.

Job Title	DOT #	GED Req M / L	SVP Req
Chauffeur Funeral Car	359.673	1 2	4
Explosives Truck Driver	903.683	1 2	3
Log Truck Driver	904.683	1 2	4
Dump Truck Driver	906.683	1 1	2
Deck Hand	911.687	1 1	4
Automobile Detailer	915.687	1 1	2
Tow Truck Operator	919.663	1 2	3
Driver	919.683	1 1	3

    Refer to pages 71 to 72 in Selected Characteristics
of Occupations from the Dictionary of Occupational
Titles (U. S. Department of Labor, 1981) for the
complete listing of jobs within this Work Group.

INTEREST AREA 05 MECHANICAL

OAP 25   Q 085   K 085
GOE 05.09   MATERIALS CONTROL

Workers in this group receive, store, and/or ship materials and
products. Some estimate and order the quantities and kinds of
materials needed. Others regulate and control the flow of materials
to places in the plant where they are to be used. Most have to
keep records.

    Refer to pages 110 to 114 in the Guide for Occupational
    Exploration.

Job Title	DOT #	GED Req M / L	SVP Req
Marker	209.587	1 1	2
Booking Clerk	216.587	1 1	3
Checker	221.587	1 2	2
Odd Piece Checker	221.587	1 2	2
Recorder	221.587	1 2	2
Grey Goods Marker	229.587	1 2	2
Ticketer	229.587	1 2	2

    Refer to pages 73 to 75 in Selected Characteristics
of Occupations from the Dictionary of Occupational
Titles (U. S. Department of Labor, 1981) for the
complete listing of jobs within this Work Group.

INTEREST AREA 05 MECHANICAL

OAP 26   S 085   P 080   M 085
GOE 05.10   CRAFTS

Workers in this group use hand and handtools skillfully to fabricate, process, install, and/or repair materials, products, and/or structural parts. They follow established procedures and techniques.

Refer to pages 115 to 122 in the Guide for Occupational Exploration.

Job Title	DOT #	GED Req M / L	SVP Req
Sand Blaster, Stone	673.382	1 1	6
Engraver I	979.381	1 2	5

Refer to pages 77 to 84 in Selected Characteristics of Occupations from the Dictionary of Occupational Titles (U. S. Department of Labor, 1981) for the complete listing of jobs within this Work Group.

INTEREST AREA 05 MECHANICAL

OAP 27   P 080   K 085   M 085
GOE 05.10   CRAFTS

Workers in this group use hand and handtools skillfully to fabricate, process, install, and/or repair materials, products, and/or structural parts. They follow established procedures and techniques.

Refer to pages 115 to 122 in the Guide for Occupational Exploration.

Job Title	DOT #	GED Req M / L	SVP Req
Saw Setter	701.684	1 2	5
Repairer	709.684	1 2	5
Carpet Layer Helper	864.687	1 2	3
Glass Installer	865.684	1 2	4
Circular Saw Operator	869.682	1 2	5

Refer to pages 77 to 84 in Selected Characteristics of Occupations from the Dictionary of Occupational Titles (U. S. Department of Labor, 1981) for the complete listing of jobs within this Work Group.

INTEREST AREA 05 MECHANICAL

OAP 28   S 085   P 080   M 085
GOE 05.11   EQUIPMENT OPERATION

Workers in this group operate heavy machines and equipment to dig, drill, dredge, hoist, or move substances and materials. They also operate machines to pave roads.

Refer to pages 123 to 126 in the Guide for Occupational Exploration.

Job Title	DOT #	GED Req M L	SVP Req
Core Drill Operator	689.682	1 2	5
Bulldozer Operator	850.683	1 2	5
Power Shovel Operator	850.683	1 1	5
Road Roller Operator	859.683	1 1	3
Derrick Operator	921.663	1 1	4
Hoist Operator	921.663	1 2	4
Pneumatic Hoist Operator	921.663	1 1	3
Derrick Boat Operator	921.683	1 2	5
Dump Operator	921.685	1 1	3
Tractor Operator	929.683	1 1	3

Refer to pages 85 to 87 in Selected Characteristics of Occupations from the Dictionary of Occupational Titles (U. S. Department of Labor, 1981) for the complete listing of jobs within this Work Group.

INTEREST AREA 05 MECHANICAL

OAP 29   K 085   M 080
GOE 05.12   ELEMENTAL WORK: MECHANICAL

Workers in this group perform a variety of unskilled tasks, such as moving materials, cleaning work areas, operating simple machines, or helping skilled workers.

Refer to pages 127 to 135 in the Guide for Occupational Exploration.

Job Title	DOT #	GED Req M L	SVP Req
Sandwich Maker	317.684	1 1	2
Cook Helper	317.687	1 1	2
Kitchen Helper	318.687	1 1	2
Refrigrtn Mechanic Helper	637.687	1 2	2
Auto Body Repairer Helper	807.687	1 1	2
Painter Helper, Automotiv	845.684	1 1	4
Blaster Helper	859.687	1 1	3
Tile Setter	861.684	1 2	2
Pipe Fitter Helper	862.684	1 2	3
Tire Repairer	915.684	1 1	3
Steam Cleaner	915.687	1 1	2
Rigger Helper	921.687	1 1	3

Refer to pages 89 to 98 in Selected Characteristics of Occupations from the Dictionary of Occupational Titles (U. S. Department of Labor, 1981) for the complete listing of jobs within this Work Group.

APTICOM A5   PAGE 12

NAME: JACK STAGG   ID#: 007   DATE: 6/5/86

VOCATIONAL RECOMMENDATIONS
BASED UPON
ADJUSTED APTITUDE SCORES

Listed below are additional Work Groups which you may wish to consider. Although you do not "technically" qualify for these Work Groups there is the possibility that your attained aptitude scores underestimate your true aptitude. You must also recognize, however, that your adjusted scores may overestimate your true aptitude.

INTEREST AREA 04 PROTECTIVE

    OAP 16   G 095
    GOE 04.02   SECURITY SERVICES

Workers in this group protect people and animals from injury or danger. They enforce laws, investigate suspicious persons or acts, prevent crime, and fight fires.

   Refer to pages 68 to 69 in the Guide for Occupational
   Exploration.

Job Title	DOT #	GED Req M___L	SVP Req
Police Officer	375.367	1 2	5
House Officer	376.367	1 2	4

   Refer to pages 39 to 40 in Selected Characteristics
   of Occupations from the Dictionary of Occupational
   Titles (U. S. Department of Labor, 1981) for the
   complete listing of jobs within this Work Group.

INTEREST AREA 05 MECHANICAL

    OAP 21   S 090   P 085   M 085
    GOE 05.05   CRAFT TECHNOLOGY

Workers in this group perform highly skilled hand and/or machine work requiring special techniques, training, and experience.

   Refer to pages 88 to 100 in the Guide for Occupational
   Exploration.

Job Title	DOT #	GED Req M___L	SVP Req

   It is recommended that you meet with your vocational counselor.

   Administrator Note: See Tech Message E 1

   Refer to pages 53 to 65 in Selected Characteristics
   of Occupations from the Dictionary of Occupational

Titles (U. S. Department of Labor, 1981) for the complete listing of jobs within this Work Group.

INTEREST AREA 05 MECHANICAL

OAP 22   N 090   S 090   P 085
GOE 05.07   QUALITY CONTROL

Workers in this group inspect and/or test materials and products to be sure they meet standards.

    Refer to pages 104 to 107 in the Guide for Occupational Exploration.

Job Title	DOT #	GED Req	SVP Req
		M____L	

It is recommended that you meet with your vocational counselor.

Administrator Note: See Tech Message E 1

    Refer to pages 69 to 70 in Selected Characteristics of Occupations from the Dictionary of Occupational Titles (U. S. Department of Labor, 1981) for the complete listing of jobs within this Work Group.

INTEREST AREA 05 MECHANICAL

OAP 24   G 095   N 085   Q 090
GOE 05.09   MATERIALS CONTROL

Workers in this group receive, store, and/or ship materials and products. Some estimate and order the quantities and kinds of materials needed. Others regulate and control the flow of materials to places in the plant where they are to be used. Most have to keep records.

    Refer to pages 110 to 114 in the Guide for Occupational Exploration.

Job Title	DOT #	GED Req	SVP Req
		M____L	

It is recommended that you meet with your vocational counselor.

Administrator Note: See Tech Message E 1

    Refer to pages 73 to 75 in Selected Characteristics of Occupations from the Dictionary of Occupational Titles (U. S. Department of Labor, 1981) for the complete listing of jobs within this Work Group.

APPENDIX H

CAREER EVALUATION SYSTEMS REPORT

The following system dedicated report is only one of four report formats available as part of the Career Evaluation Systems' assessment process. The length is largely dependent on the number of jobs included in the printout. This report was based on a seven hour evaluation of a client referred by a private-for-profit rehabilitation counselor, to determine his feasibility for services (placement and/or training program). The evaluation was conducted by Easter Seal Rehabilitation Center in San Antonio, Texas, and the resulting report processed on the Career Evaluation Systems' computer in Niles, Illinois, by telecommunication. Although the format allows for personal comments, in this case, the center developed its own narrative report to accompany the printout. It should also be noted that this client received an additional 18 hours of assessment prior to a full evaluation report being written.

Report provided by:

    Career Evaluation Systems, Incorporated
    Niles, Illinois
    Ann Williamson, Vice President
    and
    Easter Seal Rehabilitation Center
    San Antonio, Texas
    Joe De La Cruz, Director of Rehabilitation

CAREER EVALUATION SYSTEMS, INC.
7788 MILWAUKEE AVE., NILES, IL 60648
SERIES 200 - STANDARD JOB EXPLORATION

6061 Easter Seal Rehab Center
Date of Test:05/20/86 (Entry: 05/27/86)   RSA code(s) a)399 b)   c)

Client Name:FICTITIOUS ANNA   ID.No.CES-AF-0002
Sex:Female   Age:40   Race:Caucasian   Years of Education:12   Spec. Ed.: 0
Dominant Hand:Right   Specific Voc. Prep.:Up to Two Years

Basic test scores entered: T1/ 15   T2/ 18   T3/ 13   T4/ 172   T5/   4
       T6/ 51   T7/ 75   T8/   3   T9/   4   T10/ 3   T11/CNT   T12/DNG
       T13/DNG   T14/DNG   T15/DNG   T16/DNG   T17/ 17   T18/ 30   T19/DNG
       T20/ 8   T21/ 4   T22/559   T23/ 97   T24/ 85   T25/ 6   T26/ 31
       T27/ 28   T28/ 11   T29/ 5   T30/ 39   T31/ 27   T32/148   T33/ 21
       T34/ 50   T35/DNG   T36/ 59   T37/ 59   T38/ 35   T40/ 5

Comments:

```
                                   --------RATINGS  DISTRIBUTION--------
                                    1.0      2.0      3.0      4.0      5.0      6.0
                                    VERY              LOW      HIGH              VERY
TEST PERFORMANCE          Rating    LOW      LOW      AVG.     AVG.     HIGH     HIGH
Unilateral motor ability
   FINGER DEXTERITY        5.0      ----------------------------------->
   WRIST-FINGER SPEED      4.0      --------------------------->
   ARM-HAND STEADINESS     5.0      ----------------------------------->
Bilateral motor ability
   MANUAL DEXTERITY        4.0      --------------------------->
   TWO-ARM COORDINATION    4.0      --------------------------->
   TWO-HAND COORDINATION   4.5      ------------------------------->
   HAND-TOOL DEXTERITY     1.0      -->
   MULTI-LIMB COORD.       0.0 DNG
   MACHINE FEEDING         0.0 DNG
Lifting ability
   HAND STRENGTH           2.0      ----------->
   LIFTING ABILITY         0.0 DNG
Perceptual
   PERCEPTUAL ACCURACY     3.0      ------------------->
   PERCEPTUAL SPEED        3.0      ------------------->
   SPATIAL PERCEPTION      4.0      --------------------------->
   DEPTH PERCEPTION        0.0 DNG
Perceptual-motor coordination
   AIMING                  4.5      ------------------------------->
   REACTION TIME           2.0      ----------->
   FINE PERC-MOT.COORD.    5.0      ----------------------------------->
   VISUAL MOTOR REVERSAL   5.5      ------------------------------------->
Intelligence
   ABSTRACT REASONING      2.0      ----------->
   VERBAL REASONING        4.0      --------------------------->
   NUMERICAL REASONING     2.0      ----------->
   DECISION SPEED          2.0      ----------->
   RESPONSE ORIENTATION    6.0      ------------------------------------------->
   ORAL DIRECTIONS         4.0      --------------------------->
Achievement/Ability
   READING LEVEL           6.0      ------------------------------------------->
   ARITHMETIC LEVEL        3.0      ------------------->
```

DATA NOT CONSIDERED:

Multi-Limb Coord.	Machine Feeding	Lifting Ability
Depth Perception		

GED =   2.8

Physical Limitations
   Light Lifting
   No Climbing
   No Continous Stooping
   No Extensive Standing
   Very Limited Reaching

Environmental Limitations
   No Continuous Cold
   No Continuous Wet/Humid
   Minimal Hazards

D.O.T. Category: DATA Ratings
  0.. SYNTHESIZING   3.2 100%
  1.. COORDINATING   3.2 100%
  2.. ANALYZING   3.2 100%
  3.. COMPILING   4.0 100%
  4.. COMPUTING   3.5 100%
  5.. COPYING   4.0 100%
  6.. COMPARING   2.9 100%

D.O.T. Category: PEOPLE Ratings
  .0. MENTORING   2.0
  .1. NEGOTIATING   2.0
  .2. INSTRUCTING   5.0
  .3. SUPERVISING   5.0
  .4. DIVERTING,ENTERTAINING   2.0
  .5. PERSUADING,SALES   5.0
  .6. SPEAKING,SIGNALLING   4.0
  .7. SERVING   4.0
  .8. FOLLOWING DIRECTIONS   4.0

D.O.T. Category: THINGS Ratings
  ..0 SETTING UP AND ADJUSTMENT   3.8 100%
  ..1 PRECISION WORKING   4.6 100%
  ..2 OPERATING-CONTROLLING   4.1 90%
  ..3 DRIVING-OPERATING   4.0 73%
  ..4 MANIPULATING   4.2 100%
  ..5 TENDING   3.8 95%
  ..6 FEEDING-OFFBEARING   3.9 75%
  ..7 HANDLING   3.0 63%

THIS PROGRAM IS PROTECTED UNDER COPYRIGHT LAWS OF THE UNITED STATES AS AN
UNPUBLISHED WORK. COPYRIGHT 1986, CAREER EVALUATION SYSTEMS, INC.

SPECIFIC FEASIBLE JOBS

D.O.T. CODE/PAGE	TITLE	GOE CODE	L	GED	SVP
976.382-026 s28	COMPUTER-OUTPUT-MICROFICHE OPERAT	05.10.05	1	3	2
215.563-010 172	CALLER	07.07.03	0	2	2

SPECIFIC POSSIBLE JOBS

D.O.T. CODE/PAGE	TITLE	GOE CODE	L	GED	SVP
261.357-030 208	SALES REP TEXTILES	08.02.01	0	3	4
299.357-014 221	TELEPHONE SOLICITOR	08.02.08	0	3	3
109.367-010 s08	MUSEUM ATTENDANT	07.04.04	1	3	3
205.367-062 s14	REFERRAL CLERK, TEMP. HELP AGENCY	07.05.03	0	3	3
215.367-022 172	TIMEKEEPER	07.02.05	1	2	3
221.367-058 182	REPRODUCTION ORDER PROCESSOR	07.05.03	0	2	3
221.367-066 182	SCHEDULER MAINTENANCE	07.05.01	0	2	3
237.367-022 192	INFORMATION CLERK	07.04.04	0	3	4
237.367-050 193	TOURIST INFORMATION ASSISTANT	07.04.04	0	3	4
249.367-082 s15	PARK AIDE	07.04.03	1	3	3
296.367-010 219	AUTOMOBILE LOCATOR	07.05.03	0	3	3
379.367-010 s17	SURVEILLANCE-SYSTEM MONITOR	04.02.03	0	3	2
249.387-022 203	READER	07.05.02	0	2	1
556.130-018 s18	MOLDING SUPERVISOR	06.02.01	1	3	5
550.135-014 s18	MIXING SUPERVISOR	06.02.01	1	3	5
249.167-014 201	DISPATCHER MOTOR VEHICLE	07.05.01	0	3	3

CONCEIVABLE JOBS

D.O.T. CODE/PAGE	TITLE	GOE CODE	L	GED	SVP
970.661-014 933	LETTERER	01.06.03	0	3	6
209.667-014 640	ORDER CALLER	05.09.03	1	2	2
209.667-010 164	COPY HOLDER	07.05.02	0	3	4
349.677-018 s16	CHILDREN'S ATTENDANT	09.05.08	1	2	2
359.677-030 s17	RESEARCH SUBJECT	09.05.06	1	2	1
970.681-014 933	COLORER	01.06.03	0	3	3
078.687-010 063	LABORATORY ASST. BLOOD AND PLASMA	02.04.02	1	2	2

APPENDIX I

MESA REPORT

The following system dedicated reports are an example of two of the report options available from the MESA (Microcomputer Evaluation and Screening Assessment) system. The reports are based on a four and-one-half hour assessment (including report writing time) of a back injured worker referred by a state compensation commission to determine his residual functional capacity. A summary report and worker qualification profile analysis are presented, and although additional comments can be added to the reports, they were not included in these printouts.

Reports provided by:

VALPAR International Corporation
Tucson, Arizona
Donald R. Ross, Ed.D., Vice President
Director, Product Development

Valpar International
MESA 84

```
                         MESA
                  EVALUATION SUMMARY

            Valpar International Corporation
                    3801 E. 34th St.
                       Suite 102
                  Tucson Arizona 85713
                    (602) 790-7141
                   Charles J. Rastatter
```

JOHN J. DOE
Sex: M   Age: 33   Grade: 16
Occupation: METER READER
Referred by: STATE COMP
Date: 2-Jul-86

Distinguishing Characteristics:

BACK INJURY

The Evaluee has distinguishing characteristics which may require
consideration for more specialized evaluation. You should
review the results of MESA carefully to determine if they have
been affected in any way by these characteristics.

MR. DOE WAS REFERRED FOR EVALUATION IN ORDER TO DETERMINE
RESIDUAL FUNCTIONAL CAPACITY.

              SCREENING EVALUATION RESULTS

    A 'D' means the Evaluee's score is based on untimed
    academic exercises.

ACADEMIC SKILLS   GRADE LEVEL

    Mathematics   9
    Vocabulary   10+
    Spelling   10+
    Reading   14

PERCEPTUAL/ NEUROLOGICAL

	Percentile
Vision Screening	95
Size Discrimination	40
Shape Discrimination	90
Eye-Hand Coordination	60
Eye-Hand-Foot Coordination	30
Color Discrimination	High

MANUAL DEXTERITY/ MOTOR COORDINATION/ TOOL USE

	Percentile
Block Assembly	65
Hammering	25
Alignment/ Driving	85
Block Disassembly	85
Wobble Board - Bolts	95
Machine Tending	95

FINGER DEXTERITY/ FINE ASSEMBLY

	Percentile
Wobble Board - Screws	95
Fine Finger - Dominant	95
Fine Finger - Non-Dominant	95
Wiring	95

PHYSICAL CAPACITIES

STRENGTH

Lifting	80 lbs.
Hand Grip	150 lbs.
Palm Press	50 lbs.
Horizontal Press	110 lbs.
Vertical Press	50 lbs.

Page 3   DOE, JOHN J.

GENERAL MOBILITY

Walk Forward	Yes
Walk Backward	Yes
Heel/Toe	Yes
Walk/Toe	Yes
Walk/Heel	Yes
Balance Right	Yes
Balance Left	Yes
Squat	Yes
Climbing	Yes
Kneeling	Yes
Crawling	Yes
Stooping	No
Crouching	No

GENERAL ABILITY

Problem Solving	High
Visual Memory	Average
Reasoning Ability	High
Instruction Following	High Avg
Talking/ Persuasive	High
Independent Perceptual	High

VOCATIONAL INTEREST

GUIDE FOR OCCUPATIONAL EXPLORATION (GOE)

02	Scientific	High
03	Plants/ Animals	High Avg
05	Mechanical	High Avg
08	Selling	Average
07	Industrial - Support	Average
10	Humanitarian	Average
01	Artistic	Average
11	Leading/ Influencing	Average
12	Sports	Average
06	Industrial - Production	Low Avg
09	Accommodating	Low Avg
04	Protective	Low

Page 4   DOE, JOHN J.

VOCATIONAL INTEREST FACTORS

1st Choice:	Communication of Data	1b
2nd Choice:	Processes/ Machines/ Technical	4b
3rd Choice:	Tangible/ Productive/ Satisfaction	5b

VOCATIONAL AWARENESS   High Avg

DOT PROFILE SUMMARY

An asterisk (*) means the Evaluee's upper or lower limits have not been tested in that specific area.

An L means the Evaluee's score is not based on MESA or Valpar Work Sample scores.

An X means the Evaluee's score is inconsistent.

D	P	T	GOE	Phy Dem	Work Cond	GED R	M	L	SVP	Int	Temp
2	2	4	02	V2-456	B	5	4	4	7	1b4b5b	RV

APTITUDES

G	V	N	S	P	Q	K	F	M	E	C
2	2	2	2*	2L	2	3	3	2	3	2*

SUMMARY AND RECOMMENDATIONS

MR. DOE SHOULD BE REFERRED FOR CAREER COUNSELING IN ORDER TO SELECT JOB POSSIBILITIES THAT ARE COMPATIBLE WITH HIS RESIDUAL FUNCTIONAL CAPACITY.

Evaluator: DONALD ROSS

2-Jul-86

Valpar International
MESA 84

```
            DICTIONARY OF OCCUPATIONAL TITLES
              WORKER QUALIFICATION PROFILE
                       ANALYSIS

            Valpar International Corporation
                    3801 E. 34th St.
                       Suite 102
                 Tucson Arizona 85713
                    (602) 790-7141
                  Charles J. Rastatter
```

JOHN J. DOE
Sex: M   Age: 33   Grade: 16
Occupation: METER READER
Referred by: STATE COMP
Date: 2-Jul-86

Distinguishing Characteristics:

BACK INJURY

The Evaluee has distinguishing characteristics which may require
consideration for more specialized evaluation. You should
review the results of MESA carefully to determine if they have
been affected in any way by these characteristics.

MR. DOE WAS REFERRED FOR EVALUATION IN ORDER TO DETERMINE
RESIDUAL FUNCTIONAL CAPACITY.

                       PROFILE ANALYSIS

The Worker Qualification Profile analyzes the subtests of MESA
as they relate to the Dictionary of Occupational Titles' worker
functions of Data, People, and Things, and to the worker trait
factors of Physical Demands, Work Conditions, General
Educational Development (GED), Specific Vocational Preparation
(SVP), Aptitudes, Interests, and Temperaments.

The Evaluee's results reported here can be compared directly to
the skill levels required for specific local job, classroom, or
training situations for which an Access Profile has been
established.

An asterisk (*) means the Evaluee's upper or lower limits have
not been tested in that specific area.

An L means the Evaluee's score is not based on MESA or Valpar
Work Sample scores.

Page 2   DOE, JOHN J.

EMPLOYMENT/EDUCATIONAL BACKGROUND

MR. DOE HAS COMPLETED FOUR YEARS OF COLLEGE AND WAS EMPLOYED AS A METER READER FOR JONES LIGHT AND POWER AT TIME OF INJURY.

WORKER FUNCTIONS

The worker functions relate to the level of performance of the Evaluee to the job/worker situations related to Data, People, and Things.

DATA	CLASSIFICATION
Skills with intangible data such as numbers, symbols, ideas, and concepts.	2

PEOPLE	
Skills with People (includes animals when dealt with as human.)	2

THINGS	
Skills with Inanimate Objects (machines, tools, equipment, etc.)	4

VOCATIONAL INTEREST

GUIDE FOR OCCUPATIONAL EXPLORATION (GOE)

02	Scientific	High
03	Plants/ Animals	High Avg
05	Mechanical	High Avg
08	Selling	Average
07	Industrial - Support	Average
10	Humanitarian	Average
01	Artistic	Average
11	Leading/ Influencing	Average
12	Sports	Average
06	Industrial - Production	Low Avg
09	Accommodating	Low Avg
04	Protective	Low

DOE, JOHN J.

PHYSICAL DEMANDS

Physical Demands relate to the Evaluee's physical capacities to do work.

1.	Strength	V - Very Heavy
2.	Climbing/ Balancing	Yes
3.	Stooping, Kneeling, Crouching, and/or Crawling	No
4.	Reaching, Handling, Fingering, and/or Feeling	Yes
5.	Talking/ Hearing	Yes
6.	Seeing	Yes

WORK CONDITIONS

Work Conditions relate to the Evaluee's preference of location of work site and environmental factors (other than normal.)

1a.	Inside	Yes
1b.	Outside	Yes
2.	Extreme Cold	No
3.	Extreme Heat	No
4.	Wet and/or Humid	No
5.	Noise and/or Vibrations	No
6.	Hazards	No
7.	Atmospheric Conditions	No

GENERAL EDUCATIONAL DEVELOPMENT (GED)

GED relates to education (both formal and informal) which contributes to the Evaluee's Reasoning, Mathematical, and Language development. Level 6 is High, Level 1 is Low.

Reasoning Development	5
Mathematical Development	4
Language Development	4

Page 4   DOE, JOHN J.

SPECIFIC VOCATIONAL PREPARATION (SVP)

SVP relates to the amount of time the Evaluee has determined to spend to develop the necessary skills for a career.

SVP   2 to 4 years.   7

APTITUDES

Aptitudes relate to the level of the Evaluee's specific capacities or abilities which facilitate learning of tasks or of job duties. Level 1 is High. Level 5 is Low.

#		Aptitude	Level
1.	G	Intelligence	2
2.	V	Verbal Aptitude	2
3.	N	Numerical Aptitude	2
4.	S	Spatial Aptitude	2*
5.	P	Form Perception	2L
6.	Q	Clerical Perception	2
7.	K	Motor Coordination	3
8.	F	Finger Dexterity	3
9.	M	Manual Dexterity	2
10.	E	Eye-Hand-Foot Coordination	3
11.	C	Color Discrimination	2*

VOCATIONAL INTEREST FACTORS

1st Choice:	Communication of Data	1b
2nd Choice:	Processes/ Machines/ Technical	4b
3rd Choice:	Tangible/ Productive/ Satisfaction	5b

TEMPERAMENTS

Temperaments relate to the Evaluee's adaptability for specific types of job/ worker situations. (Listed in order of strength).

Repetitive/ Continuous	R
Variety/ Change	V

Page 5   DOE, JOHN J.

ADDITIONAL WORKER CHARACTERISTICS

Additional worker characteristics important to job success. Level 2 is High. Level 4 is Low.

INSTRUCTION FOLLOWING

Evaluee's level of ability to follow
written and/or oral instructions.   2

VOCATIONAL AWARENESS

Evaluee's general awareness of the
world of work.   2

The Evaluee has demonstrated a very high level of ability in the areas listed below. You should consider additional evaluation to determine the Evaluee's upper performance limits in these areas.

AREA

S - Spatial Aptitude
C - Color Discrimination

SUMMARY AND RECOMMENDATIONS

MR. DOE SHOULD BE REFERRED FOR CAREER COUNSELING IN ORDER TO SELECT JOB POSSIBILITIES THAT ARE COMPATIBLE WITH HIS RESIDUAL FUNCTIONAL CAPACITY.

Evaluator: DONALD ROSS

2-Jul-86